Grace

From Joyce to Grace

Grace Neils Woodbridge

ISBN 978-1-0980-2198-6 (paperback)
ISBN 978-1-0980-2535-9 (hardcover)
ISBN 978-1-0980-2199-3 (digital)

Christian Faith Publishing, Inc.
832 Park Avenue
Meadville, PA 16335
www.christianfaithpublishing.com

Printed in the United States of America

To my husband, Timothy, who inspired and encouraged me to write the book. Without your moral support, your love and encouragement, it would have stayed in my to-do list. Thank you!

To my children, my pride and joy, Roger, David, and Debra. My children are an inheritance from the Lord.

And Jesse, Ra, and Nia, my grandchildren.

God's reward.

Dear Reader,

I want to acknowledge my Trinidadian (Trini) style of speaking. This is reflected in my writing.

Contents

Acknowledgements

The Holy Spirit

I give honor and glory to God, the Holy Spirit, for guidance, inspiration, and help to write this memoir. I couldn't do it without God's help.

Timothy, my husband.

I want to thank you for encouraging me and believing in me. Standing with me in the days and months it took me to write this memoir. Encouraging me to take breaks and go for walks.

Roger Clarke, my son.

Your support and encouragement was outstanding, connecting me with Chrome and helping me to write the document; you made the process possible. The times that you reached out to me and said, "Mom, write the book! You can do it!" Thank you!

David Clarke, my son.

You were there for me from the start of the book. When I declined to find out about my ancestors, you inspired me to send for the kit. You were a light that shined so brightly, that showed me the way and brought light into my life when I found out about my heritage from my DNA, and found home.

Karen, my therapist.

I want to let you know how much you have helped me to overcome the fears and the feelings of abandonment and loneliness that had followed me from my childhood. The months that I had stopped and couldn't go on, your counsel helped me to move forward and complete this memoir.

The Title of My Book, How I Was Inspired to Write My Book

The title for my book was inspired by my husband. I had shared with him my difficult childhood, and that I was called by the name Joyce and how I found out Joyce wasn't my name, and he said from Joyce to Grace. We looked at each other and together said, "That's it!" Write the book. That's the title of the book, *From Joyce to Grace.*

When I looked back at my life experiences and saw where I came from and where I am now and how I overcame the obstacles that life presented me, and I am still standing, I realized that there might be many people who had similar experiences, and by sharing mine, it would help them to know that they weren't alone and also inspire them to want to write their own story and set themselves free like I have been set free. Also, there are people who may not yet experience the hard and difficult challenges of life, but my story may be a compass to let them know someone went through what they might be going through and came out a winner, not a loser, and find their purpose in their story.

I want my story to inspire, motivate, and encourage people and to let them know it doesn't matter what adversity comes their way; they don't have to go under. They can rise to the top and be whatever they want to be at whatever age they may be, and as long as they are standing, they can make it successfully in life. I did it. I am their mentor to encourage them to never give up hope. There is a payback, and life will pay back whatever was stolen from them.

Overview

At the age of fifteen, I was raped by a man that lived in a common-law marriage and had children in the marriage. He deceived me and took my virginity. I had no knowledge of sexual interactions. Sex without consent is rape. It wasn't until as an adult, I came into the knowledge of what rape is when I did a research on rape and saw that it is any act of nonconsensual sexual penetration. It doesn't matter if the victim was raped by force or under duress, the crime is still rape, and that is what he did to me. I never had a father's love, and when he took an interest in me, it made me feel accepted, and I trusted him. In a way, I was looking to this man for the affection that I didn't get from my father. I grew up without a father's affection or mother's or any form of affection from any of my family or relatives. In Trinidad, even in the mid-1900s, molestation and rape weren't words that were known by most Trinidadians.

Rape is a crime of violence. Rape isn't sex for the person being raped. I was a teenager when I was raped. It was very traumatic. I wasn't yet a young adult, and my life came to a halt. I was a mother before I was a woman. I heard that a female becomes a woman at the age of twenty. I was a mother at the age of sixteen and still wasn't a woman. Rape robbed me of my education and accomplishing things that teenagers do and enjoyed. Instead, I was raising an illegitimate child. In Trinidad, in the mid-1900s, there wasn't the option of continuing school after giving birth to a child. There wasn't a child day care once you become a mother. My life as a teenager was finished. At sixteen and with a child, I was considered to be a woman. I was a child holding down two jobs, one in the evening and the other in the daytime. I went to bed after midnight and awoke early the next morning to start my day job. I was only sixteen. Rape denied me the chance to make my own life decisions. It chose a life for me and set me on a course in life that I didn't choose. I lived with anxiety, a sense of helplessness, and persistent fears and phobias. I missed out on having teenage friends, instead I was a mother.

I didn't have the opportunity to enjoy my teenage years, celebrate life, or attend a prom school-night celebration. Where I was living, I couldn't remain. I had to leave, and I had no place to live. Through an acquaintance I met a man at a Unitarian gathering; he took me in to live at his apartment, and I lived in a cohabited relationship. He became very abusive and controlling, and I was pregnant, and life seemed hopeless. I was just functioning in the relationship, doing the daily work activities, the cooking and cleaning. I was trapped, and there seemed to be no escape. I was afraid to leave and to be on my own with my son. I was insecure, and I submitted to the life that I was living. I felt like a prisoner. It wasn't until I came to a place many years later, when I couldn't go on any longer living as a battered wife, that I got divorced. I took classes, and I completed my education. I was on my own, a single mother raising three children. I was a battered wife, divorced, and a single parent. My beginning didn't dictate my future. I was born an illegitimate child. I was molested at four years old.

When I was seventeen and working to support myself and my child, I was raped twice by the son of the owner of the business and had two abortions. I went through a difficult life. It started at the age fifteen, but by the grace of God, I am still going on strong with a passion for life and a purpose.

* * * * *

Trinidadian speech is characterized by dropped final consonants and a lack of pluralization. There is no standard orthography for the written language; written forms which attempt to capture the sound of the language tend to converge. There is a wide variety of cultures and nationalities of people found in Trinidad and Tobago. These two are the most cosmopolitan islands in the Caribbean, with a very diverse population that is mostly African and East Indian in origin, but that includes Syrians, Chinese, Americans, Europeans, and Parsees. But they all speak English with a Trinidadian accent.

From Joyce to Grace,
Beginnings

When a child is not nurtured or given the emotional environment for healthy development or attachment and has to hide who she is to be accepted and not be rejected, emotional abandonment happens. That child feels isolated, utterly forsaken, insecure, abandoned, and anxious. The child loses the ability to connect to other people because abandonment interferes with the ability to trust others. When the people who take care of her are suddenly gone without explanation, suddenly no longer there, and this is the pattern of her childhood, the foundations for trust are never put into place. Real trust becomes impossible. Fear sets in, and anxiety attachment becomes overwhelming.

When she is in another person's care, she feels unsafe and doesn't know whether that person will remain in her life. She becomes withdrawn and introverted. Feelings of a lack of control, loneliness, and rejection can come from having been unloved as a child. As an adult, that child may continue to feel abandoned and unlovable in all relationships. That child was me.

Childhood

I was born in the Caribbean, in Petersfield, Chaguanas, Trinidad and Tobago. I was called Joyce from birth, but that wasn't my name. When I began writing my story, I realized I had no knowledge of my ancestors, and I was encouraged by my son, David, to have my DNA tested to discover where my ancestors came from. Although reluctant at first because I thought it wouldn't matter or be important, I finally sent for it. I registered with Ancestry DNA, followed the instructions, activated the kit online, mailed in the sample, and waited. The results came back showing that my ancestors were brought to Trinidad as slaves from the Kingdom of Dahomey, now Benin, on the West Africa coast. I am descended from an African kingdom that lasted from 1600–1900.

I am also a mix of Ghana, Mali, Nigeria, Southern Bantu, Western and Central India, and Portuguese.

I am the first child born out of wedlock, the daughter of Christine Neils Gould and Ishmael Hamilton. My dad, Ishmael, met my mother, Christine, and fell in love with her, but my paternal grandmother didn't like her and didn't want her son to keep company with her, so she sent him off to serve in the Trinidad and Tobago army. But not before my mother was pregnant with me, her first child. She gave birth while my dad was away. I was raised by my maternal grandmother, Laura Neils, whom I called Tanty. She took me after I was born, and my mother went to work as a live-in maid. Although I have ten half-siblings, I am an only child for my mom and dad. I never met my maternal or paternal grandfathers.

Tanty, my grandmother

Kindergarten

At five years old, I was enrolled in kindergarten at Chaguanas Government Public School. I was taken to school by my grandmother. She dropped me off and left, and for the first time I was in a classroom with children I didn't know. I had never before been away from my home. I was frightened and terrified. I felt deserted and alone and I didn't talk with the other children. I cried and cried all day. And again the next day, I cried and cried. After the third day, I stayed by myself. I did not mix with the other children, and even now as an adult, I don't make friends easily. Every afternoon at recess, milk and cookies were given after we played games and returned back to class. Once a month, on Friday, a nurse came to the school and gave us an oil laxative; it tasted nasty. Many of the children resisted taking it, but it was given to them, and the school was closed for the day.

In the first grade I had an embarrassing experience. Four of us were sitting at a desk across from each other. The teacher said, "No talking!" One of the boys sitting across from me reached under the desk and put his hand on my knee. I pushed his hand away and told him to stop it, but just at that moment the teacher turned around. He called me up to the front of the class. He didn't ask why was I talking, and he didn't give me space to tell him. He pulled me and put me across his lap and spanked me on my behind with his bare hands as the children watched. I felt humiliated. I started to cry, and I walked back to my seat. This unhappy experience, being spanked in school, can still hurt me even at age 74, some 65 years later: such is the power of corporal punishment in schools.

School

In 1955, Princess Margaret visited Trinidad. The students of Chaguanas Government Primary School were taken and lined up along Churchill Roosevelt Highway to wave to her our welcome. I was one of those students. I will never forget: she, graceful, elegant, petit, standing in the vehicle as it passed by and waving with her small and delicate hands in white gloves as we waved back with our flags in our hands.

I was sent to live with my great-aunt Erica, my maternal grandmother's sister who worked as a domestic. She was an excellent cook. She lived on a hill, and every evening after school, I sat in the gallery (in Trinidad a porch is called a gallery) and saw her coming home walking up the hill. I would run down the hill to meet her, and when she got home, we had dinner. I stayed with her for a short while.

I lived with my maternal grandmother, Tanty, for a while and then went back to my aunt Sybil whom I began to call Mama. I was back and forth between Mama and Tanty. When Tanty couldn't afford to take care of me, she sent me back to live with Mama. When Mama lived in Arima, she was living with Uncle, and every Sunday morning, he got up early and went to the store to buy a newspaper and bananas. He always took me with him, and when we got back to the house, I was given a whole banana. That experience stayed with me all my life, and when I became an adult, I bought bananas every time I went to the grocery store. Even now, I have bananas every day. This is funny. When I got married, I found out my husband also likes bananas, and together we have a banana every day.

I lived with my great-aunt Erica in one place, aunt Mama Sybil in three places, and with my grandmother Tanty, four places. These being Couva, Montrose, Chaguanas, Arima, Petersfield, Chaguanas again, Enterprise Village, and Port of Spain. I never lived with my mother, which is why I called aunt Sybil Mama.

Petersfield, Chaguanas

My grandmother had six children: three sons, Sidney, Samuel/Sam, and Knolly; and three daughters, Christine, Sybil, and Evelyn. Uncle Sidney had two sons, Mervin and Eric, my cousins, but later he had three daughters. My grandmother left downtown Chaguanas and we went to live in Petersfield at my uncle Sidney's, her eldest son's, house. She had her own bedroom, and there were other bedrooms where my cousins, Mervin and Eric, slept but there wasn't a bedroom for me. So I slept under my grandmother's bed on bedding. Every morning, I took the bedding out and hung it in the sun, and at night I took it in and made my bed under my grandmother's bed.

Children were always told by the adults that the bogey-man or the Jumby man would get them. I told myself that I didn't know who the buggy man was, but he sounded scary to me, and if he comes into the house at night, he won't see me under the bed, so I felt safe.

To take a bath, I boiled water and poured it into a bucket with cold water. Using a calabash bowl (made from a gourd) I poured the water over my head. I used shampoo and soap, and then rinsed with the water. The latrine and bath were outdoors behind the house. There was no electricity in the village. We used Kerosene oil lamps and every morning I cleaned the lamps of soot and refilled them.

It was my responsibility to take the chamber pot out in the morning to empty and wash it and take it back into the house to be used again that night. I was afraid of the dark, and there were times I forgot to bring it in before it got dark. I would be terrified and stricken with fear. I couldn't see it, but I knew where I had left it. I would search around, find it, and then run quickly back into the house.

The village public water station was a quarter-mile away, and every morning before I left for school, I walked and fetched water at the station. I made a couple trips back and forth, carrying buckets of water to cook, wash clothes, drink and bathe. It was a happy time when it rained. My grandmother had a barrel under the waterspout where the water ran off and when it rained the barrel filled up with water that we used to wash clothes and to bathe. I collected the water for drinking and cooking. I enjoyed bathing in the rain with other family members and friends who joined in from the neighborhood as we played catch me if you can. When it rained, it fell heavily over the eaves from the roof of the house, and we stood under as the water poured down over our heads. Wide ditches ran alongside the roadway to catch the rain; they were too wide to jump across and each house needed a bridge to cross over to the road.

Rainy season in Trinidad runs from June to December. In the rainy season, mornings are usually sunny followed by rainy afternoons and fair nights. There are times when the rain continues for days and nights, the sun comes out for a short time, and then the rain continues. On dark nights

I loved watching the stars as they twinkled so brightly. On moonlit nights it seemed bright as daytime and I could see the trees and the fruit on the trees. There are many fruit trees, over fifty various kinds. I loved to climb them and sit between two branches and read. One of the books I enjoyed reading was *The Basket of Flowers: A Tale of the Young*, written in 1878 by Christoph Von Schmid, and when I wasn't reading, I liked to ride my bike. My favorite fruits were mangoes, cashews, pomegranates, soursops, sapodillas, guavas, bananas, kimit. One of the neighbor's sapodilla fruit trees was off limits to us, and she didn't give away her sapodilla fruits. Her tree was full and laden with sapodillas, and she didn't pick them. She was in advanced age and stayed indoors; I never saw her outside. There were times when my cousins and I waited at night for her to turn off her lights and go to bed. We climbed the tree and picked the sapodilla fruit, and when she heard us, she shouted at us from her window, and we ran away. On moonlit nights, Mervin, Eric, and I were allowed to stay out longer than our regular bedtime hours, and we challenged each other to see how many stars we could count.

There were hundreds upon hundreds and so beautiful. Some nights we played hide-and-seek and listened to each other as we ate fruit and told stories. Other times we crossed the street into the sugarcane field, broke off a piece of sugarcane, and chewed it. Those times were special, both looking at the stars shining in the dark sky, and on bright, moonlit nights when the whole village was lit up like daytime at night and I could see my cousins as we sat outside in the yard and talked. On dark nights we said it was pitch-dark, like the darkness of the asphalt of the street. Then you could barely see your hands or a person if you were outside with someone.

Felicity, in Chaguanas, then and now, is little more than a few mile's stretch of main road. Then, houses ran along one side of the road, with space between them. The other side was taken up with sugarcane fields, and workers traveled many miles to work in them. They got up early, starting work at 6:00. My grandmother Tanty got up every morning at 4:00 to cook lunch for Uncle Knolly, her third son. She packed his lunch in a three-tier lunch box which kept the food warm, made him breakfast, and sent him off to work. She was very close to him, her baby boy child whom she adored. When he returned home after work, she had a light meal waiting for him. At that time in Trinidad, dinner was served at noontime, and in the evening we had tea and a light snack.

When Uncle Knolly met Rose and fell in love with her, I was nine years old. She lived with us and helped his mother with the cooking and food preparation. She gave birth to their first child, Joanne, and became his common-law wife. They have four daughters and two grandchildren. Uncle Knolly died in 2018 at the age of eighty.

St. Hilda's Anglican School

My grandmother moved from downtown Chaguanas to nearby Enterprise Village. We stayed there for a short time and then moved to Lastique Street, East Dry River, Port of Spain, to her daughter Evelyn's home. I was enrolled at Piccadilly Government Primary school, Port of Spain, and the next year, I attended St. Hilda's Anglican coed all-girls school on Quarry Street. I wore a navy blue overall uniform, blue socks, short sleeves white blouse, blue tie, black shoes, blue or white ribbons. Every morning, before leaving home for school, I washed the breakfast dishes, which I did not like doing and did other household chores. I did this every morning before I had breakfast, took a bath, and dressed for school. I had very thick long hair, and I did not know how to plait it, and every morning I waited on Tanty to comb and plait my hair. Sometimes she kept me waiting while she did other things. Almost every day, I ran to school. I couldn't be late.

The school was gated with a high brick stone wall around it. I had to be on time, and if I were late in the morning or late returning from lunch, I would find the gate locked. There was one entrance into the school, and when the gate was locked, I had no way to get in and had to return home. There are times I just made it in; just as the gate was closing, I got there. One day, I was waiting on my grandmother to plait my hair and was thinking, "When would she comb my hair?" I couldn't tell her that I was ready for school or ask her when she would plait my hair; to do so would be considered rude. While I waited, I began twisting and twisting my hair, and I learned how to plait my hair and tied the ribbons. The next day, I continued twisting my hair, and I discovered that I can plait my hair, and I became very creative, styling it in various ways and took great pride doing it. From that moment, I never waited on my grandmother to plait my hair; I did it myself. We weren't allowed to take lunch to school, and at noontime, we were given an hour for lunch and sent home. There wasn't a food cafeteria or snack machine at school.

Tanty was a hard-working woman; she cooked lunch every day for Uncle Sam, one of her sons, who worked in the dry cleaning laundry business as a *pressor* on Charlotte Street. At lunchtime, I ran home, had my lunch, and took Uncle Sam's lunch to his job half a mile and back to school. I ran so that I won't be late getting back to school, and I did this five days a week. As a child, I could not understand why the gate had to be locked, but now that I am older and wiser, my thoughts are, the school was a two-story building. There was no bell at the gate, and for the children's safety, it was locked, so no one could enter unannounced. Every morning, the class had fingernails inspection before class begins. Students formed a line on the school grounds and extended fingernails to be inspected. If nails were dirty, the teacher took a wooden ruler, and the students were hit on their fingernail which was very painful.

One day, I was told to stand on a chair in the middle of the class. The teacher made a paper hat which she called a dunce hat and put it on my head because I did not get the subject correct. She did this to other students as well. The school building was made in such a way there was an opening under the roof that lets air in, and anyone walking outside on the sidewalk could see me standing on the chair as the students looked on giggling.

Cousin

My cousin, Janet, Aunt Sybil's daughter, lived with her father, and we didn't get along. We were far apart in age. Tanty raised me. She cared for me since birth. She was attentive to me, and Janet was jealous. Tanty loved her just as she loved me. I had a very long hair, and sometimes Janet would say to me, "You think you're better than me because of your long hair?" Anytime I was in her company, we fought terribly with each other. I was told as a child that my paternal grandfather was from East India Madras, which is now called Chennai. When I received Ancestry DNA results, it didn't say Madras but from Western and Central India (Indians came to Trinidad as Indentured Servants), a land of both seaports and deserts with a history that stretches back to the ancient Indus Valley Civilization.

One day, Janet came to visit our maternal grandmother, but Tanty was away at the market in Port of Spain where she went every Saturday morning to buy fruits and vegetables. Tanty's life was wrapped up in her two sons, Uncle Knolly and Uncle Sam. She spent her life at home and indoors, but she looked forward to going to the market on Saturdays, and that's where she seemed very happy. Sometimes she took me with her, but this Saturday, she went alone. When Janet, my cousin, came to visit, she waited for Tanty to return from the market. We were talking as she waited, and we had an argument. She got angry, threw things, and I ran out of the house while she ran after me. I ran to the neighbor's house, and she stopped and went back to the house. Janet had a love-hate relationship with me. Sometimes she was nice, and other times she wasn't. There were times she came over to visit, and if I wasn't at home, she missed me and would ask my grandmother, "Where is Joyce?" She thought that Tanty liked me more than her. Janet couldn't deal with the thought of Tanty's affection for me.

Her dislike for me was not valid, and her thinking that our grandmother liked me more than her was wrong. In some ways, we were like sisters when we weren't fighting. When Tanty came home, I came back from the neighbor's and nothing was said about what happened. There were many other times Janet and I fought for stupid things, but when she got violent, that was it. It was all in her head that Tanty liked me more than her because Tanty did not treat Janet any different than the way she treated me.

Tanty's Laundry Business

I lived with my grandmother on Lastique Street, East Dry River, Port of Spain, at her daughter Evelyn's home. My grandmother had no friends. She was a very private person and kept secrets to herself. No one came to visit her, nor did she visit anyone. Tanty had a laundry business when we lived in Port of Spain. She had a few clients, and sometimes business was slow. She took five days to complete washing the clothes. In Port of Spain, we had electricity and running water outdoors and indoors with a faucet and a kitchen sink (where I washed dishes) but no indoor shower or bathroom. We had a latrine, and bathing was done outdoors in a covered hut. Outside had a pipeline and a faucet where water was collected in a bucket and put into the washtub with a scrubboard for washing clothes; this was how Tanty washed her customers' clothes. On Mondays, she washed the clothes by hand in a large washtub with a scrubbing board and then laid them in the sun on a wire rack to sun bleach. From time to time she poured water over the clothes so that the sun wouldn't dry them out, and she'd leave them out overnight on the wire rack.

Tuesday mornings, she took the clothes off the wire rack and washed them again, then put the clothes back on the wire rack in the sun and repeated what she did on

Mondays. Then she picked them up, rinsed them, and hung them to dry. On Wednesdays, she boiled starch, put the starch liquid in water in the tub and the clothes in the starch water, and rinsed them and hung them to dry. On Thursday, she sprinkled the clothes with water, wrapped each piece separately, and put them in a big container overnight. On Fridays, she ironed the clothes. She put charcoal into a coal pot (like a small barbecue grill). She lit the coals and put the clothes' iron on the hot coals, and she ironed the clothes one by one. On Saturdays before market, I delivered the clothes to her customers and collected the money, or her clients picked them up. That's the way she saw her mother do it. And I thought it doesn't take that long a time to wash clothes.

When I washed my clothes, I put them in the washtub and washed them with hard block soap, rinsed them the same day, starched them and hung them on the clothesline to dry, and the next day I ironed them. Tanty didn't like the way I washed my clothes, and she always fussed with me, telling me that my clothes weren't clean. I had a mind of my own, and I saw things differently than she did, so we didn't get along in that area. Tanty was a woman of principle. She lived by a strict set of rules and schedules and knew what to do on specific days and time. I had problems with her strict schedules, and many times I would be disciplined. I couldn't understand why she took such tedious time to do a job that could be done in one day. I admired her ways but always looked for the easiest way to do a job. We had many disagreements, and there were times when she would say, "Joyce, you will never learn how to wash clothes. I feel sorry for that man you will marry."

Life with Tanty

When we lived on Lastique Street in Port of Spain, Tanty drank Nescafé Coffee every morning. They came in single packs; that was the only coffee she drank. If a morning she was out of coffee, she'd send me to the corner store to buy more. She never started her day without it. At night, she had hot organic all-natural chocolate, the kind that came in blocks. She'd grate chocolate and put it into a cup and pour hot water into the cup. Tanty had gray hair; it runs in the family. My mother was fully gray in her adult years, and my uncle Sam, me, and my sister Angela. Angela keeps her gray hair; she doesn't color it and it looks so beautiful; she loves it. For many years, I color rinsed my hair. I went to the hairdresser twice a month. I stopped coloring my hair, and I am enjoying my beautiful gray.

Tanty didn't like her gray hair, and she made her own color rinse. She took charcoal and ground it into powder and mixed it with coconut oil and made a paste to cover her gray hair. At night, she covered her head with a head wrap and went to bed. She had specific ways of doing things, and one of her disciplines was that I should wear a different outfit for every occasion and event. I had clothes to wear inside and outside, for bedtime, play, school, church, recreation, and other events. When I came home after school, I changed into play clothes. I didn't dare wear my school clothes for play, and now as an adult, I have the same habit. I don't wear the same clothes that I wear outdoors indoors. As soon as I came home from outdoors, work, shopping, or church, I had to change into my indoor clothes before I did anything.

Another discipline my grandmother taught me was to pray before I went to bed, and prayer time was after I had my bedtime snack and brushed my teeth, and not before. That habit continues in me even now. My ancestors' genes live in me; my ancestors alive in me even now.

One day, Tanty took me to an event in a park in Chaguanas. There were music, games, candy canes, and lots of other treats for children. I was playing and I stumbled and fell. My dress ripped from the waist and my knees were all bruised; I started to cry. I was sure that I would get a beating but I didn't. The event was over and we went home. I washed up and changed into my pajamas, said my prayers, and went to bed. The next day, Sunday morning, when I got ready to choose my dress for church, she gave me the ripped dress and I wore that to church. But I asked myself this question, "Why did she do that?" Even now I don't know.

When I did something wrong I'd get a spanking. Tanty would say, "Get the belt," and I would get it and give it to her. My cousin, Janet, was different; she didn't get the belt. She ran out the house and stayed out for a while, and when she came back, she had forgotten about spanking. Tanty got the belt, and she was spanked.

Angela

My mother had eleven children, ten half-siblings after I was born. My sister, Angela, was the second child, and my brother, Jeffrey, was the third child. My mother had four more children in a common-law marriage and four more after that in a civil marriage. I was raised by my maternal grandmother, Tanty, and my sister Angela by her godmother. And although we both lived in Chaguanas, we did not know each other in our childhood. Once, I was told where she lived in Chaguanas and I went to visit her. I was eight years old, and she was seven. I met with her godmother. She invited me in the house and gave me milk and cookies, but I was not allowed to spend time with my sister. She was doing her chores. I waved at her and left. I felt hurt I didn't get to talk to my sister, and as I am writing my memoir, the memory of how I felt begins to surge within me, and I begin to feel the pain and the child within me cries for her sister. I did not get to see my sister. I felt the hurt and the pain; it hurts even now; and I broke down crying. I didn't block it.

My sister, Angela

I let myself cry as I kept saying I missed my sister. I missed my sister. As the tears flowed, I didn't hold back. My husband had said to me, "Don't block any of your feelings or emotions. Just let it go. Cry if you feel like crying, get angry if you feel anger." Also that, "It will get rough as you stir up all those hurt experiences, but don't block them." When my husband came home and saw me crying, and I told him what I was experiencing, he hugged me and said to me, "I wish I can do something to make the pain go away." And I said, "You're doing something by comforting me." Then we lay on the bed as he embraced me, and I began to feel better. This was the second time I broke down writing my memoir as the pain of my passed life experiences began to overwhelm me. The first time I stopped writing and took a couple months off before I could resume writing. When I saw my sister, Angela, again, she was married and had two children, a boy and girl, my niece and nephew whom I hadn't met until they were eight and nine years old. When I went back to Trinidad for two weeks' vacation, I was like a stranger to them.

I lived with my grandmother (Tanty) in four places, including Port of Spain. Then I left Trinidad and I did not see Angela again for twenty-six years. From an early age, my sister Angela was used as child labor. She had to clean her godmother's house, take care of the chickens, sweep the yard, do the cooking, feed the pigs, and more. She had limited education—though years later she completed it—and was not given playtime. She had full adult responsibility. And she became an excellent cook. She cooks for family and friends, and caters parties for weddings and church events, sometimes for hundreds of guests, and most of the time she does it alone. She makes and sells achar with mango and tamarind, tamarind balls, hot pepper sauce (which is her specialty). She gets many orders from people who like her hot sauce and order large amounts.

When her friends' families visit from America, before they arrive they send orders for large quantities for her to make that they can take back with them. She makes dhalpuri roti, pholourie eaten with mango chutney; pastelles and more. Whenever I visit, I take home two kinds of achar, sweet and hot, dhalpuri roti, and other cooked items. Her house is always spick and span, and she has an exceptional taste for designing a home. My niece, Dianne, and nephew, Andre, Angela's children, grew up and have children of their own. Andre, her son, has a boy and a girl and one grandson; Dianne, her daughter, has four daughters and twelve grandchildren. My sister and I have a close relationship. She lives in Enterprise, Chaguanas. We talked every week by phone or Skype. We are very close. Whenever I visit Trinidad, Angela and my brother, Jeffrey, pick me up at the airport and I stay at her home. We were separated as kids, but by God's grace we were connected.

Mother

I am the first and only child for my mom and dad and was not acquainted with my half-siblings. I knew my mother had given birth to other half-siblings before and after I left Trinidad, and they lived in Chaguanas with her. Some of them were very young and didn't know me at all. I left Trinidad in 1967 and did not return until 1980. I spent two years in Canada, relocated to America, and I didn't have legal status to travel abroad. When I came back to visit Trinidad, it was different from when I left. There was now the Uriah Butler Highway, when before I had traveled from Chaguanas to Port of Spain on local back roads. I didn't recognize Trinidad. I felt like a foreigner, completely lost. When I had lived with my mother and had my first son, Dexter, she lived in Felicity, Chaguanas, and before I left Trinidad, I took Dexter to live with her in Petersfield, Chaguanas.

When I came back in 1980 to visit her, she had moved to St. Thomas Village, Chaguanas, and I saw my half-siblings. They were like strangers, and I didn't know who they were. One of my brothers was standing next to me, and I said to him, "Who are you?" And he said, "I'm your brother, Patrick." As time went by, a few of my half-siblings came to America. We live in different states and have limited communication. My mother moved to Chrissie Terrace, Enterprise, Chaguanas, where she lived until she died. Whenever I visited Trinidad, I spent time with my sister, Angela, and my mother. I slept over in both places and spent time with them. In December 2016, I went to my mother's ninetieth birthday party. All her grands and great-grands got together and gave her a big birthday party celebration. They invited all her children those near and afar, her friends and relatives; there were over two hundred attendees.

My mother was a friendly, forgiving, and giving person. She held no malice. If someone offended her, she certainly let them know how she felt. But once she did so, she let go the offense. She was very generous with her children and grandchildren, and whenever they had a need, she gave to them and did without. When she laughed, the air filled with her laughter. She can be heard from a distance. She loved life. She had a ruptured varicose vein near her ankle and it was very painful for many years, and walking was difficult. She came to America to visit and had received treatment but wasn't healed. In her later days, she spent most of her time at home, taking care of her grandchildren, great-grand, and great-great-grand. Her home was always filled with her grandchildren, and she loved having them around. Then came the day when she could no longer walk and was bedridden.

My mother

Angela took her food every day for several years and helped her with things that she wasn't able to do. In February 2018, I received a call from my sister, Angela, that she wasn't doing well. She had no taste for food and didn't eat much. The next day, I booked a flight to Port of Spain and spent two weeks with her. She loved reading the Bible; her favorite scriptures was Psalms, but she could no longer read or sit up in bed. She told me the scriptures that she read, and I read them to her. The day before I returned back home, Angela and I prayed with her. I gave her communion, and I told her I loved her, and if we don't see each other again, we will meet again in heaven. On April 18, 2018, Angela called me and said she had passed six weeks after I came back home. She loved children and had a ministry to children. Every year, she had a feast for them. She cooked and fed the children in the community. The first year after she died, my sister, Angela, cooked and fed the children in her remembrance.

My mother was born December 26, 1926. She had thirty-three grandchildren, fifty-one great-grandchildren, and twenty-one great-great-grandchildren, a combined total of one hundred and five. She lived to be ninety-two years. I will always cherish those memories and the times we spent together as I read her favorite Bible scriptures when she called out the ones she loved to read, and I read them to her. Psalm 91 was one of the scriptures she asked for.

Jeffrey

My brother Jeffrey is two years younger. As a child, I saw him a couple times when he was twelve. We both lived in Petersfield, Chaguanas, when I lived with my grandmother. I left Chaguanas with my grandmother and went to live in Port of Spain. In 1967, I moved and went to live in Montreal, Canada and in 1970 I relocated to Boston, Massachusetts. We knew each other but it wasn't until we were adults and I went back to vacation in Trinidad that we saw each other again. He invited me out to a restaurant, and we had dinner. I ate curry chicken, Pelau, coo-coo, and callaloo, with sorrel drink, with his wife and my niece; she was six years old. Whenever I visit Trinidad, I can always depend on Jeffrey to pick me up at the airport, even late at night. When I am ready to leave, he drives me to the airport. And when I was invited to visit family members in San Fernando, he took me. We don't communicate regularly, but he's always been available to help me when I'm there.

Saturday Cleaning

Every Saturday, my responsibility was cleaning my grandmother's apartment. We lived on the first floor of her daughter's, my aunt Evelyn's, house on Lastique Street, Port of Spain. My aunt lived upstairs with Uncle Joe in a common-law marriage. She had six children. On Saturdays, I took everything out that could be moved outdoors, the chairs and table, and I cleaned and polished them. I took the bed linen, hung them on the clothesline, and the linoleum on her floors I cleaned inside, and I put everything that I took out back into the apartment and set them the way they were. Saturday mornings when my grandmother went to the market she'd sometimes take me with her. She bought meat and fish and put them in the fridge that replaced the ice box in Chaguanas. We no longer lived in Chaguanas and had no access to food grown on the land, breadfruit, bananas, dasheen, sweet potatoes, cassava, and other vegetables, and meat bought at the abattoir. On the days that she took me, I did the house cleaning in the afternoon when we came back from the market, and the days that it rained, I cleaned indoors. On days that I didn't go with her, I did the cleaning in the morning.

Washing dishes was one of my daily assignments morning and evening, which I dislike. My grandmother loves to cook many varieties of food, cassava/yucca bread, pone, and farine cereal, also paime and pastelle and more. There were many dishes used, and whenever I went out to play and came back, the sink would be piled high with dirty dishes.

Train Ride

Train ride from Chaguanas to Port of Spain to visit Aunt Gladys, my great aunt, my grandmother's sister who lived on St. Vincent Street, Port of Spain. Whenever she went to visit her sister, she took me with her. We went to the train station terminal at Gasparillo Junction and boarded the train to Port of Spain. On the ride, we passed cows and other animals grazing in the field. Water buffalo were bathing in the swampy water, some standing while others lay down on the grass chewing their cud and watching as the train went by, passing houses and the trees' leaves blowing in the wind under the blue skies. Wisps of clouds going by as the moving train rolled along. I stood by the window next to Tanty enjoying both the ride and the scenery. I never forgot the train ride; it was a pleasure and exciting experience. When the train arrived in Port of Spain, we got off and walked to Aunt Gladys's home. She was always happy to see her sister. She gave us food and we slept over.

The next day, when Tanty got ready to leave, we took a taxi to the train station terminal and boarded the train for Chaguanas and took a taxi to Felicity. When Tanty and I moved from Chaguanas to live in Port of Spain, she visited her sister more often.

Trinidad and Tobago Railway ran from 1876 to December 28, 1968. Chaguanas was named for the Chaguanas Amerindian tribe. The area was settled by the time of the British conquest of Trinidad in 1797 and is the largest borough and fastest-growing town in Trinidad and Tobago, located in west-central Trinidad, about twenty-five miles south of Port of Spain.

Group Excursion

When I lived in Port of Spain, on a school vacation, Tanty and Aunt Evelyn planned a bus excursion to a park before school resumed. Eleven of us went. Auntie, Tanty, me, Auntie's four children, and four neighbor children. They rented a bus, and we drove for two hours to the park. The park had trees, benches, and hills in a wide-open space. The night before, the adults stayed up and cooked food for the trip. The kids were sent to bed early, and we were awakened about four in the morning. They made pelau, curry chicken, dhalpuri roti, and macaroni pie. They took fruits, mango, pomme-racs, chennette, sorrel, and mauby juice. The next morning, we had a light breakfast and got dressed as they packed the food and drinks in a basket. The bus driver arrived about 5:00 a.m., and it was very dark when we boarded the bus, so we went back to sleep. We continued to sleep as the sun rose, and we got up and got out when the bus arrived at the park.

The adults found tables with benches and covered the tables with tablecloths while we went running and playing all over the park. They put the snacks on the table and called us to give us fruits and sweets that they had brought.

At noon, we got together with them and had lunch. After lunch, we went back to play. We lay on the grass and rolled back and forth on a hill that wasn't steep. Mid-afternoon we were called back for another snack, and at about four p.m. the adults packed the baskets with the empty bowls and other items and got us ready to get back on the bus and head home. We didn't sleep on our way home; we sat together, looked out the window, and talked. When we got home, we helped to take the baskets inside. I said my good-byes and then took a bath and got ready for bed; it was a fun day, and I was very tired.

Culture

The distinct cultures that have a major influence on Trinidad and Tobago culture are the Indian, African, Portuguese, Amerindian, Spanish, and Chinese. Afro-Trinidadians make up the country's largest ethnic group with approximately 36.3 percent of the population being of mostly African descent (Indians from India the second largest). Trinidad is the third wealthiest nation in the western hemisphere. Place of my birth, a cosmopolitan country, Trinidad is a beautiful place, the land of the hummingbird, with many beaches and botanic gardens. Over fifty fruit trees grow in different seasons, and fruit is always available almost everywhere in Trinidad. And vegetables like pumpkin, cassava, dasheen, eddoes, melongene, lettuce, tomatoes, avocado/zaboca, pimento, carrots, cucumber, scorpion pepper, and many others. The land of Calypso music and Carnival. Jump-up Jouvert Monday morning is the start of Carnival. Sunshine and warm weather under ninety degrees all year, sometimes cooler, but never cold.

My grandmother was born in the late 1800s. At the time, common-law marriage was practiced in Trinidad. My early childhood was not a typical middle-class environment.

I was born in a culture where common-law-marriage was common. My grandmother lived in a common-law marriage. She had six children. All six lived in common-law marriages, but one of the six also had a civil marriage. Marriage practice varies greatly in Trinidad among ethnicity and class. There are four stages, nonresidential relationship, Cohabitation, followed by common-law marriage and finally formal marriage. A common-law marriage is one that is formed through agreement rather than through the license and solemnization that are necessary to contract a ceremonial marriage. Yet the common-law marriage, once formed, is deemed by the law to be real. A common-law spouse has the same rights and obligations as a married one. I gave birth to two children out of wedlock. I lived in cohabitation relationship for a period of time and finally a formal marriage.

Herbs and Fruits

In Trinidad, there are many fruit trees, and fruit grows abundantly. It's like a fruit paradise. In New England, in the summer, the leaves are green. In the autumn seasons, various shades of leaves turns into New England fall foliage colors. I loved to ride through the scenic countryside and see the displays of nature, the different shades of red, purple, yellow, orange, and the beautiful blends, red, yellow, orange, and gold. Where I lived in New England, the first year I kept looking for fruits on the trees. The leaves turned into beautiful colors, but there were no fruits. After the second year, I asked, "When would the trees bear fruits?" And I was told that the trees didn't bear fruit. I was so accustomed seeing trees with fruits; it was a culture shock, and after a while, I grew to accept the change. In Trinidad, there are many fruits, coconut, portugal, peewah, pommerac, sapadilla, chataigne, cashew, oranges, and more. We dried the orange skin, and made tea, to relieve stomach discomfort. When one fruit tree was out of season, there was always other fruit trees blooming.

The fruit trees bear fruits both in season and year-round. Growing up as a child in Trinidad, I enjoyed picking and eating the fruits. I climbed the trees and picked the mangoes, and I shake the tree branches, and many mangoes fell to the ground. On windy days, many mangoes were blown off the trees and fell to the ground. There are many kinds of mangoes, Julie mango, calabash mango, rose mango, starch mango; there was always mangos in season. I enjoyed mango and coconut. I ate curry mango, green mango, ripe, in chutney in chow, and achar. While some mangos were ripe and ready to be picked, other trees were just budding with mangos. Whenever I visited Trinidad, my sister Angela always had mangoes prepared for me. There are three different types of coconuts, tall coconuts (typica), dwarf coconuts (nana), and hybrid coconut. They are used to produce both coconut oil and coconut water. There were many ways that I enjoyed coconut; I ate coconut soft jelly and in the raw, coconut molasses Tulum, coconut sugar cake, and bread. The coconut was grated to make coconut oil which was used for skin, body, hair care, and cooking.

As the years go by, the availability of fruit is diminishing. There aren't as many mango trees, and other fruits are not as common as they once were.

When I lived in Petersfield Village in Chaguanas, the home was fenced around with red hibiscus shrubs that bloomed beautifully all year. There are hibiscus flowers in a variety of colors, including pink, red, yellow, white, and multicolor. Hibiscus is a perennial and grows yearly. As a child, I brushed my teeth with the stem of the hibiscus plant. Every morning, before I did my chores, I broke off the plant stem, removed the skin, and chewed it until the ends were fluffy. This was my Trinidad toothbrush. The stem is medicinal, curing a variety of illnesses, and whitens the teeth. In east Africa, the stem is called "mswaki" in

Swahili, the word for toothbrush. I didn't have a modern toothbrush, and I didn't need one. Hibiscus gives many benefits and medicinal properties. It relieves colds. It has minerals and vitamin C. It has active flavonoids. I ate the flowers and made hibiscus tea. The hummingbirds and butterflies can be seen hovering over the flowers. There are many medicinal herbs in Trinidad to cure various sickness and body discomforts.

My grandmother and aunt knew exactly what kind of herbs to use for herbal healing and to cure various illness. Different kinds of herbs grew on the land with the corn trees, pigeon peas trees, vegetables, and other herbs that grow from the bushes, grasses, and trees. There were shining bush, carpenter's grass, turmeric. Ginger was dug out of the ground. Senna grows on the bush, and the aloe vera plant. There were different kinds of herbs, edible herbs, herbs for cooking and medicinal uses. When I lived in Chaguanas as a child there wasn't a clinic or doctor's office. Midwives helped the women during labor, delivery, and after the birth of their babies. I was pregnant with my first child, Dexter, and I didn't have maternity doctor's visits or care. The first time I was seen by a doctor was when Dexter was born at Port of Spain General Hospital.

I was raised in a holistic community. Medicinal use of plants began in Trinidad and Tobago with the first inhabitants, Amerindians from northeast South America. Their indigenous treatments were supplemented by European explorers and settlers, starting in the fifteenth century, then by slaves from Africa and later by indentured laborers from India and Southeast Asia.

Church

I was baptized as an infant at St. Thomas Anglican Church in Chaguanas, Trinidad. My grandmother dressed me in an all white head bonnet, dress, and baby booties. But I had no knowledge of this or what was happening, nor how I would be connected to this many years later. I was confirmed at the age of seven, and again wore all white. It was a very exciting time. I had an understanding of what was happening. I attended confirmation classes with other children and we were prepared for confirmation day. The day arrived when we were taken to church. We kneeled as the priest prayed, and we repeated the prayer after him. We had communion and were sent home. There wasn't any celebration. I mistakenly thought that I was a Christian because I had this experience; I had completed the confirmation process. There were times I was asked whether I was a Christian and I said yes. However, I found out it's by grace; we are saved through faith. No class or confirmation can replace this requirement. I came to the realization and knowledge that until I made the decision for Christ and was born again, I wasn't a Christian.

As a child, I didn't understand the christening/baptism celebration as the newcomer was welcome to the family.

As I grew older, I came to understand the customs for infants, baptism, the parties and dancing, and the celebration given by the guardian or parents of the child as family, friends, and neighbors got together, played parang music (Christmas soca), and ate. And many different kinds of dishes were cooked: rice and beans, callaloo souse, mauby juice, sorrel, ginger beer (which has no alcohol), and homemade ice cream. Soursop fruit (milky white flesh) ice cream was made with coconut cream mixed with milk and put into a nonelectric bucket ice cream maker, which all the children took turns churning by hand, turning the crank even as it became ever harder to turn. When the ice cream churn became stiff, the adults took over. They covered the ice cream bucket and left the ice around the bucket to keep the ice cream hard until it was ready to be served. We were given the ice cream churner to clean with ice cream stuck onto it and got the first taste of the ice cream. When my grandmother and I moved from Chaguanas to live in Port of Spain, we attended the Trinity Cathedral church at 30 Abercromby Street, Port of Spain. Every Sunday, we walked a mile from Lastique Street, East Dry River, to church. After a while, my grandmother stopped going to church, and I continued to go alone.

As I look back, I became aware of the age difference between me and my grandmother, the aches and pain that she might have experienced, the distance that we walked back and forth, and the Sundays that it rained. I wasn't aware of how she might have felt then because she loved going to church and didn't attend. I thought maybe she didn't go because of the distance that we walked. When I attended church together with my grandmother, I sat on the pew behind her with children of other church family members that we met there and ate candy as we talked very quietly. The priest came to the platform and stood at the pulpit in his black robe attire and prayed as the adults repeated the words after him. Then the plate was passed for the collection, we sang a hymn and left. Attending church was a special time for me as a child. I didn't understand things about God and what it meant to serve God, but I loved going to church with my grandmother on Sundays. I went to church every Sunday when we lived in Chaguanas, where it was a shorter walk. But after we relocated to Port of Spain, Tanty went for only a short while.

My grandmother raised me to attend church. I was baptized and confirmed in church, and I attended church services with my grandmother. I was in church, but church wasn't in me because I didn't know much about church. I thought of church as a place where people went to be spiritual, to feel good, and be a Christian. At a certain time in my life, I did not go, and with life responsibilities, church was far away from my mind but not from my heart. There was always a stirring in my heart that there must be more to church than what I saw in church but didn't know what it was. As I advance in life, I came to the understanding that church is not a place or a building, it's in me in my heart, and when I come together with others who believe, we are the church. The building isn't the church. When I saw in the Bible, "we are God's building," then I saw another scripture that says, "let us not neglect our meeting together," I came to the realization I have found church. It was always in me.

Christmas

In Chaguanas on Christmas Eve night, my family didn't go to bed until early Christmas morning, staying up baking fruitcake, black cake, coconut bread, pastelles, and different kinds of pastries. Christmas ham was soaked overnight (the day before Christmas Eve) and baked the next night. Christmas morning, the dining table was set with almonds, walnuts, grapes, apples, and other fruits and nuts. We did not go to church on Christmas morning. We had breakfast as a family together, fresh baked bread, sweet coconut bread with sliced ham and scrambled eggs. Cooking for dinner started early Christmas morning, pelau, callaloo, macaroni pie, different kinds of meat. *Souse* was made and juice, sorrel, mauby, ponche de creme, and ginger beer (no alcohol). The food was cooked by noon and ready to be eaten on Christmas day with friends and the parang group.

On Christmas day, a group serenaded friends, going to the homes of families, friends, or patrons to sing songs, dance, and play parang music, eating and drinking from house to house as friends joined in with the group as they left and continued on with no time limit in mind. Christmas was a time of celebration and renewal. New things were bought for the home. New curtains were made. New furniture replaced old. The adults purchased drapery material and sewed drapes for the windows and doors. "Yes, even the doors!" This was a yearly community custom. The old drapery was taken down at night, and the new was hung at the windows and doors for Christmas morning. Every home in the village had new curtains and drapes; it was like a competition Christmas morning to see the neighbor's drapes as homes were visited. New Year's Eve was different. I attended midnight New Year's Eve church service with family and friends. There was a superstition that going to midnight church service brought good luck for the rest of the year.

After the service, adults and young adults changed into party clothes that we either had made ourselves or had made for us. "We didn't wear a dress to a party twice," and we celebrated until daybreak. This was the custom. Easter Sunday morning was celebrated with the focus on the children attending church service. The children, I one of them, were dressed in new clothes made for the occasion and we were given toys. The girls received dolls, and the boys had different toys. We took them with us to church for the resurrection service of Jesus Christ. Christmas was celebrated in December, but we received our Christmas gifts on Easter Sunday.

In 2009, I spent Christmas in Chaguanas. I missed Christmas. I had been away for many years and had not experienced Trinidad Christmas after I left, but Christmas in Trinidad wasn't the same. My sister, Angela, stayed up after midnight. She baked fruitcake and other food items and cooked into Christmas morning, but the merrymaking to celebrate the season no longer existed. There were Christmas lights in a few homes, but it was like a ghost town. Times had changed, and Christmas parang in Chaguanas had changed too, Christmas parang merrymaking and celebration is now just a memory.

Tanty's Death

After I left Tanty's home at the age of fifteen, Tanty moved back to live in Chaguanas, and I didn't see her again until a few years later, and when I saw her, she was sick and dying in the Port of Spain General Hospital. I went to visit her, and as we talked, she asked how I was doing and if I was happy. I didn't want to burden her with my problems, and I said yes, I was happy. She told me she was constipated and asked if I would get her some prunes. I went to the store and bought the prunes. I gave them to her and told her that I would come again to visit. When I went back to the hospital after a couple of days, I was told by a nurse that Ms. Neils had died the day before. She had got up that morning, bathed, changed clothes, went back to bed, and never woke up, and she had such a peaceful look on her face.

She was a very quiet woman who had a difficult life but had faith and believed in God. She spent most of her life helping her children. She was always there for her sons and daughters whenever they needed her. Tanty taught me spiritual values and respect for God. She took care of me, and I was happy we spent that time together. I believed she also was very happy. She was born in the late 1800s and never talked about her ancestors or how she came to live in Trinidad and Tobago. I sent for my heritage from Ancestry DNA because I wanted to know about my ancestors. She didn't talk about her life experiences as a child, nor her homeland. When I started writing my memoir, I had no knowledge of her life. I was told that she came from Portugal by my cousin, Janet, and that's what I believed before I began writing my story. When I received the results, it showed the highest percent of my DNA was from Benin/Togo.

As I continued my research, I saw that my ancestors were brought to Trinidad against their will as slaves from Dahomey, West Africa, now Benin/Togo. All my life I didn't know that my maternal grandmother was a Beninese from Africa, or about my African heritage.

History

I did an internet search about the history of Christopher Columbus. According to the history I learned in school, he came to Trinidad with three ships, Santa Maria, Pinta, and Niña. I was speaking to a friend about my childhood days in school in Trinidad and Tobago. We were having a history discussion, and I mentioned Christopher Columbus discovered Trinidad in 1492 when he sailed to Trinidad with the Santa Maria, Niña, and Pinta, and he said that's incorrect. I said to him, "You're wrong. That's what I was taught in history class," and I dropped the conversation. In my search, I found and read an article in the Trinidad and Tobago Guardian written by Irving Ward, and discovered that the ships were not the Santa Maria, Pinta, or Niña as I had been taught in my childhood, but they were the Guía (El Nao), Los Vaqueros, and El Correo; history corrected.

I was taught in history class about the indigenous Amerindian tribes, the Arawak-speaking people and the Carib-speaking people that lived on the island that was part of my history. But in the 1950s the history of African slaves brought to Trinidad against their will wasn't taught in school at all. Although I had learned some of the African customs and culture from my maternal grandmother, Tanty, the head wrap, generosity, the food a diverse blend of other cultures, such as fried plantain, callaloo made with crab or oxtail with coconut milk, okra, and dasheen leaves eaten with coo-coo made with cornmeal (it must have crab), boiled plantain, cassava, dasheen, eddoes; breakfast with roast bake and buljol made with saltfish, akkra, fry bake and shark, I didn't make the connection. I was familiar with Indian customs and food, but not African food. I didn't know that it was part of my culture and heritage from my African ancestors.

When we lived in Petersfield in Chaguanas, every Saturday Tanty got up very early in the morning and went to the abattoir to get fresh meat. Many of the villagers from the community met at the abattoir. Vegetables were sold in an open market on Saturdays. The animals butchered were pigs, goats, and cows, and dishes were made with various parts of them. The pork souse was made from the pig's feet, ear, shoulder, tail, and knuckles, and the soup from the head and shoulders of the pig. Cowheel souse and cowheel soup were made with the cow's heel. Cow tripe soup is made from part of the cow's stomach; the intestines were prepared differently in a way like pork chitterlings. Chicken *souse* was made from the chicken's feet; the head and liver were also eaten. Every part of the animal and bird was eaten.

Souse is a light dish that is popular all over the Caribbean including Trinidad. It is a clear broth of pickled animal parts that is flavored with cucumber, onion, garlic, lime, hot peppers, and other spices to tenderize the meat. It is first cooked until soft and marinated with various seasonings, so it becomes pickled. The souse was served cool. Those dishes were most often sought-after at parang parties and events. Tanty bought beef, pork, goat meat, and pig's feet, just enough meat for Sunday dinner (with the pig's feet, she made *souse*). She mixed all the meat together for cooking and left it to marinate overnight, and she cooked it the next day. Sunday mornings, she got up early and cooked before we attended church, and after church, we had dinner together. This was done only on Sundays; other days we had breakfast, a big meal at lunchtime and a light meal in the evening. We didn't have meat during the week; we had saltfish and fresh fish.

On Wednesdays, the fisherman drove by with his truck and she bought fresh fish. We had vegetables grown on the land, sweet potatoes, dasheen, eddoes, plantain, and sometimes cabbage and okra. We made pelau, bhaji, and rice dishes during the week, and I loved when she cooked stewed fish with okra, vegetable, curry potatoes with chicken, stewed fish, and rice. I left Trinidad at the age of twenty-two and lived in another country that became my home, and my ties to my birthland were severed. In my childhood, I was called Dugla (a person of mixed African and Indian descent) but didn't know what it meant. I went to the Indian Diwali Festival of Lights, which symbolizes the lifting of spiritual darkness and is celebrated in the Indian culture. I was invited to attend weddings, joined in the festivals, and ate the food. I enjoyed roti and roti dhalpuri (which is my favorite), masala curry in meats, pholourie, dhal made with yellow split peas, chicken tandoori, and more.

I am Trinidadian of African and Indian descent, and I didn't made the connection before. Whenever I was asked, "Where are you from?" I say, Trinidad and Tobago. I had no knowledge of my African heritage, not knowing I am more. I am Afro-Caribbean, not just Trinidadian. I have ties with the motherland Africa. I am connected to multitudes. I received knowledge that was not known to me before, and I am looking forward to when all the tribes come together.

History and Ancestors

As a child, I lived with my grandmother and aunts in different places and never felt at home. When I became an adult, even then I never felt at home. And years later when I visited Trinidad, everything was changed. The back roads the taxis took from Chaguanas to Port of Spain were replaced by the Uriah Butler Highway, and businesses where I shopped no longer existed. My mother moved from St. Thomas to Enterprise Village, and I felt like a tourist in an unknown country and depended on my sister, Angela, to take me around Chaguanas. Raising my own children, I lived in one place for eighteen years. I had moved around so often as a child, I wanted to give my children the stability and security I didn't have. When I got divorced, the judge asked if I wanted to change my married name. I said, "No, I will keep it until my children are grown," and I no longer needed to sign permission papers sent home from school.

My children grew up and went to live on their own, but for me, home was missing. I had this feeling that I wasn't at home, but I didn't know where home was. I lived at several places in different apartments that I liked. But in my heart, I felt something was missing. I wasn't satisfied.

Something was always missing, and it never felt like home. In my Ancestry DNA results, I found out that my ancestors were from Benin, West Africa, and I started an Internet search to know more about them. As I continued searching, the missing pieces filled in and I started to feel a sense of belonging to a people and to a tribe, of membership, and what was missing wasn't missing anymore. I found home. I felt connected. Home wasn't my birthplace in Trinidad and Tobago where I was born, but with the ancestors whose tribe I was born into, my African roots. Wherever I live now, my ancestors live in me, and we are home.

I couldn't connect with Africa before I found myself in Africa through my ancestors. When I did the research, I read about how my ancestors were brought from Africa as slaves through the Caribbean slave trade to Trinidad against their will and the inhumane and brutal ways that they were treated, and I was angry. Then I reflected on the scripture that says, "Forgive," and when I read it, I knew I had to forgive, and I let go the anger. Reflection: I see my ancestors in me through my grandmother, just like I see myself in my children. My ancestors live through me in all the things that I do, what I like or don't like. Before my Ancestry DNA results, I could not have talked about my ancestors because I had no knowledge of them. But I learned it's not only my life I am living, but I am carrying my ancestors' genes, distinctive characteristics and qualities that are unchangeable, from beyond and through my grandparents to my parents and to me, that have made me as strong as I am.

I discovered from my search that during the thirteenth century, the indigenous Edo people of the west area were ruled by a group of local chieftains. By the fifteenth century, a single ruler known as the "oba" had asserted control creating the kingdom of Dahomey. Eventually Dahomey expanded to include the Niger River delta region, now the area of the Nigerian city of Lagos.

Dahomey quickly became a highly organized and prosperous kingdom, soon trading with Portuguese and Dutch traders. It was eventually nicknamed the Slave Coast due to significant trafficking through Dahomey of Africans to the Americas, especially to the slave markets of Brazil and the Caribbean. It became a French colony in the late 1800s, finally gaining full independence from France in 1960. The country's current name, Benin, was adopted in 1975. For years, anthropologists and others looked at African ethnic groups as being mostly solitary and static. However, historians now know that huge empires and kingdoms with administrations and armies, diplomatic corps and distant trading partners have long been part of Africa's fabric.

This is especially true of West Africa, where migrations conquests and intermarriage within allied kingdoms help explain why. For example, 43 percent of people from our Benin/Togo region have DNA that looks similar to the profile for the Ivory Coast/Ghana region, and 28 percent appear to have links to Nigeria (source, Ancestry DNA). To all of whom I am connected.

"If in this life only I have hoped," then I would be miserable, but I am looking forward toward that day when I am standing together with my tribe at the throne of God with my family, all my relatives in Christ, that have gone on before me and my brothers and sisters in Christ, meeting King David, a man after God's heart; Abraham, the friend of God; Isaac and

Jacob. "After this I looked, and there before me was great multitude that no one could count from every nation, tribe, people, and language, standing before the throne and before the Lamb. They were wearing white robes and were holding palm branches in their hands." (1 Cor. 15:19, KJV, Revelation 7:9, NIV).

Trinidad

When I was four, my grandmother gave me over to my aunt Sybil for a while. At that time, my aunt lived by herself. There was a man who visited her regularly that I called cousin, the practice in Trinidad then being that children addressed all adults as uncle, auntie, or cousin. Whenever he came, my aunt would leave me with him to babysit me so she could go to the market and run errands, and when she did he molested me. I was a young child and overpowered by him. I felt what he was doing to me wasn't right. When my aunt came back, he acted like nothing happened. I felt ashamed with what he was doing to me, but I didn't know how to tell my aunt. I was glad when my grandmother came and took me back to live with her at Uncle Sydney's house.

My cousin, Janet, loved going to parties, and she invited me to my first party, I was fifteen. At the party, everyone was dancing, eating, drinking, and having a good time. Francis Barclay, a friend of my cousin's boyfriend, asked me to dance. I saw Francis a couple weeks after the party and he invited me to Carenage beach and I accepted. At the beach he raped me, I was so scared. He took my virginity. And I got pregnant. When I discovered I was pregnant, I told him. He drove me to a different beach and there I sat on a rock looking into the ocean as he told me that he has children and is living in a common-law marriage, and that he was more than twice my age.

When he told me that, I felt like the life drained out of my body. I was shocked. I felt hurt, numb, and cold. My mind was blank, and I didn't want to live. I kept looking into the sea, and I felt like walking into the ocean until I disappeared into the sea. The thought came to me, "Don't do it." I felt betrayed and hurt. I started crying. I was living on Lastique Street, Port of Spain, and was ashamed to be seen pregnant by the neighbors, and I left Port of Spain and went to live with my mother in Chaguanas. I was very quiet and reserved. I spent most of my time reading books and stayed by myself. At nine months, I started having contractions. It was time for the baby to be born. My mother hired a taxi to take me to the Port of Spain General Hospital as the pain increased. It took us one hour to get there, and I was rushed to the birthing room. My baby was born at 2:00 p.m., a boy, and I named him Dexter Calvin Neils. I stayed in the hospital three days, and on the fourth day, my mother came and took me home.

The custom in Trinidad then was that mother and new-born child were not allowed to go outdoors until after one month. I stayed in the house, and at the end of the month, I took the baby out in the stroller. I stayed with my mother for three months after and went back to live in Port of Spain. Looking for a job, I had several interviews, and I found two jobs, one in the day and a night job as a waitress in a restaurant and bar from 6:00 p.m. to midnight. Sailors on weekend furlough met at the bar every Friday night.

They ordered drinks and fried chicken. They loved fried chicken and ordered in large amounts. They respected me and treated me kindly, and I enjoyed serving them. One night, one of them said to me, "What's a nice girl like you doing in a place like this?" I worked there for one year, and then I got another job working at York Restaurant on Charlotte Street, Port of Spain, as a waitress from 4:00 p.m. to 11:00 p.m.

This restaurant was bigger, and I like the atmosphere. Francis Barclay found out where I was working, and he stalked me. He came in several times. Edmond Hanes came to the Restaurant regularly. We started talking and became friends, and after work he walked me home. One night, as he was walking me home, Francis Barclay came to us and asked me to go with him, and I said no! Edmond said to him, "She said no." The next thing, both of them were fighting in the street, and I left them fighting and ran home. The restaurant closed early the next day. Edmond and I went out to a restaurant, and we had dinner and spent the evening together. It only took one time, and I found out I was pregnant with Roger, my second child. But Edmond was transferred to another job before I could tell him, and I did not seen him again until after Roger was born. I was renting from Ms. Donna, a neighbor in the same vicinity where I lived previously in Lastique Street with Tanty; she had moved from Port of Spain and went back to live in Chaguanas. I continued working at the restaurant until the baby was due. Early one morning, around 8:00 a.m., I started to have contractions.

Ms. Donna with my sons Roger
(on lap) and Dexter (standing)

There wasn't public transportation where I lived, and I walked half hour to the Port of Spain General Hospital. When I got there, I was in so much pain. I was taken to the maternity birthing room. I could not lay down on the bed. I walked back and forth in the room. At times, I curled up on the floor. I was left without medical attention, and a nurse came into the room and saw me crying out, and she slapped me in my face and said, "Shut up," and walked out the room. I couldn't shut up. I was in too much pain to keep quiet, and I cried and screamed. I was in labor for fourteen hours without anesthesia. It wasn't until around 10:00 p.m. that night, I gave birth to Roger, my second child. The next day, thoughts came into my mind to walk out of the hospital and leave my baby, but I couldn't do it. There was a love I felt that I can't describe. I couldn't leave him in the hospital. He was born with Jaundice. We stayed in the hospital for one week, and I was released and sent home. Edmond came to see the baby, and we talked for a while. I left where I was living and didn't give a forwarding address. That was the last time that I saw Edmond.

I stayed home for a couple of weeks, and when I went back to work, I was told that I was no longer needed. A friend that I worked with invited me to a Unitarian gathering in Arima. I took the bus to Arima and went to the meeting. On my way back home to get the bus, I was told that the last bus runs from Arima to Port of Spain, stopped at 8:00 p.m., and there was no bus running. Donald, one of the attendees, lived in Belmont, Port of Spain. I asked him for a ride to Port of Spain, and I walked a mile to East Dry River and got home. I was renting from Ms. Donna and didn't have money to pay the rent or for babysitting, and the next day, she gave me notice to leave. I had lost my job. I had no money and no place to live. Donald lived on Carr Street Belmont, Port of Spain, and I contacted him and told him what happened, and he told me I can stay at his place. That's how we met. We lived in a cohabited relationship, and he became very abusive and controlling. My mother found out that I was living in an abusive relationship, and she came and took me to live with her in Chaguanas. I was pregnant with David, his child, and he came to my mother's house and took me back to live with him.

Canada

In 1967, Donald went on a vacation to Canada to visit the Canadian Expo Montreal. While he was there he filed for legal status, and he invited me to join him. We weren't on good terms, and I was very indecisive whether to accept his invitation. Donald said that he wasn't coming back to Trinidad. He proposed to me and said I was to close the apartment. He sent money to buy the tickets, and I should take some of the money to buy a wedding ring and bring it. I went to the Royal Botanic Garden, Port of Spain, established in 1818, and sat on a bench surrounded by beautiful tropical flowers, orchids, hibiscus, tulips, foliage, the beautiful landscape site of trees and green shrub not knowing what I should do as I sat there pondering whether to join him. Around me was peaceful, but inside me there was turmoil. God, what should I do?

I got this impression to take Dexter to my mother, his maternal grandmother. I came to the decision that I will accept Donald's invitation to join him in Canada. I got up from the bench, and a peace came over me as I started walking home. The next day, I took a taxi and went to Chaguanas. I told her that Donald had invited me to join him in Montreal, Canada, and asked her if she will keep

Dexter, and she agreed. I gave my mother everything in the apartment, the fridge, the bed, and the furniture, everything, and a week later I booked a flight for Roger and me and packed our clothes for the trip. I wore a blue short-sleeve summer dress, and my son wore a suit that I had previously bought him, and we left for Canada. I was six months pregnant with David, my third child, when I left Trinidad and Tobago on October 25, 1967. I wasn't aware of the cold temperature in Canada, but I was told that I needed to wear a coat. The only coat that I was familiar with was a plastic raincoat (which I wore on rainy season), and I took it with me.

On the plane, as I looked out the window, the sun was shining so brightly, and the heat from the sun on the window was very hot. I could not comprehend what coldness felt like. I said to myself, "How could it be so hot inside when the sun shines through the window and cold outside?" The climate of Trinidad and Tobago is tropical, hot all year round with little seasonal variation. The maximum temperatures are about eighty-six to ninety degrees Fahrenheit in the coolest period from December to February and a little higher in the rest of the year. My mind could not process the coldness. When we arrived at the airport, the weather was thirty degrees, and Donald was waiting in a taxi for us. I had never before experienced cold and my raincoat was useless. We got into the taxi, and he took us to an apartment on Park Avenue in Montreal, where he was staying with an older Scandinavian couple named Decker. He had rented a room from them within their apartment and we stayed with them before we got our own apartment. That same night that we arrived in Canada, he had planned to visit friends that he had known from Trinidad and Tobago, who came up also for the Canada Expo and were staying in Toronto.

The raincoat I brought with me from Trinidad was a warm-weather summer plastic raincoat and was not the right coat to wear in Canadian winter. The Decker's saw my plight and gave me a brown winter coat and a pair of white boots. Roger wore a sweater over his suit. We had arrived about 4:00 p.m., a grey afternoon and it was cold but not snowing. We went back out four hours later and it was snowing heavily with almost a foot of snow on the ground. It was the first time that my son and I had seen snow. Donald took us to Toronto that same night by bus, about 350 miles. We stayed with Donald's friends for the weekend and came back to Montreal to the Decker's. At that time I was six-months' pregnant.

We stayed with them for a month, and while we were there, we got married at the church of the Ascension, a very small wedding with a couple as a witness. We were looking to rent an apartment and found one at 6000 Park Avenue. We moved into the apartment and had to buy all utilities and furnishing for it. When we were at the Decker's, I went to the Royal Victoria Hospital Maternity Clinic and made an appointment to see a doctor. At the appointment, after I was examined, the doctor told me I was anemic.

The doctor prescribed ferrous gluconate iron to be taken with vitamin B12. Also I was low in calcium and was referred to the supplemental nutrition program for women, infants, and children. Every morning, milk, orange juice, and cheese were delivered to my apartment. I continued visits for natal care once a week. Canada is cold. I wasn't used to the cold weather. It was a big adjustment for me and Roger. Living in Canada, I learned to walk fast. In Trinidad, the pace is very slow. The weather is warm, and walking is very leisurely at a slow space. When I went shopping, I saw everyone walking fast, and I wondered why. But after a few times outdoors, I joined them. It was very cold.

We were in a foreign country with no family or friends; it was very lonely. The time went by very slowly. It was January, near time to give birth. It was 2:00 a.m. early on a Sunday morning, and the pain started coming. I woke Donald up, and we went to the hospital. When I got there, they took me right into delivery. This time I had gas anesthetic. The nurses stood by my side and told me when to push and when to breathe, and David was born at 7:00 a.m. The nurse commented, "A baby boy with a big appetite." He drank three ounces of milk right after he was cleaned up.

I had complications; my red blood cells were low, and my doctor ordered a bone marrow biopsy. They kept me in the hospital for two weeks. I continued in the supplemental nutrition program for a while, and then it was stopped. When I came home with David, I didn't have a crib. He slept in the bed, but I was afraid that I might roll over on him. I had a pram that I used to take him out for walks, and I put him in it at night to sleep. He slept in it up to the time he was sitting up. Then I bought him a crib. By this time, I had money saved, and he had his own bed. He was baptized at the church of the Ascension on March 10, 1968. David was a very active child from birth, and when I took him out for walks in the park, he was always ahead of me and could cross the side street before I got there. I was concerned that I might not get to him before he entered the crosswalk. I bought a harness for him, and in that he had free range. He didn't have to walk together with me, and he loved it. I would take my sons by bus to Mount Royal National Park in the middle of the city and on a hill. There we could picnic, my children could play, and I could watch the view looking out over Montreal.

I liked taking the train in the subway and seeing it come into the station so quietly and smoothly, without sound. I loved living in Montreal. We didn't have friends, and we were far away from relatives. We lived in a French bilingual-speaking city, in a Greek-speaking neighborhood where there were mostly Greek stores and restaurants. We were in the middle of unknown territory, but I liked the country. The people were friendly with a nod of the head, bonjour, good morning, or bonsoir, good evening, or, "Ça va?" Although I didn't speak French, the mothers I met in the local neighborhood park communicated with me and their children with mine. I loved the language, but I didn't get the opportunity to learn French.

America

I came to America from Montreal in 1970 on a vacation with my two sons, Roger and David. Donald, my husband (at that time), had gone to America to find work. He found work and without telling me decided to stay. He sent for me and the children to spend a one-week vacation in America with him. I came with the intention of spending one week and returning back to Canada. When I arrived from Canada, he picked us up at the bus station and drove us to a one-bedroom apartment which he rented at Kinnaird Street, Cambridge, Massachusetts. It was a very small room, but I didn't mind. My thoughts were, "We will be there for a short while and eventually return back to Canada." His trade was plumbing, and I was happy when he told me he found work in America. Montreal is French-speaking, and it was very difficult to find a job if you didn't speak French. To my surprise, he said to me that we weren't going back to Montreal, and he has decided to relocate in America and apply for permanent residency.

I was shocked. I had no money to purchase a ticket and return to Canada, no friends or family living in America. All our belongings were in the apartment in Montreal. I had clothes for one week and my passport. The two-bedroom apartment we had in Montreal, was completely furnished with living room furniture, bedroom furniture, kitchen appliances, the children's bedroom fully furnished, everything that I had acquired for two years. My son, David, was born in 1968 at the St. Elizabeth Royal Victoria Hospital in Montreal, and was two years old and in daycare, and my son, Roger, who traveled with me from Trinidad was seven years old and attending school in Montreal. I was working at a clothing and apparel establishment, registered to take a French course after work to learn French and be bilingual (which I was excited about), and I would have started the week after I returned back to Canada. I hadn't expected to remain in America and didn't made preparation for closing the apartment or storing our belongings, and I didn't know what to do. There wasn't a botanic garden to visit and to decide what I should do.

Donald was very abusive, demanding and controlling. When I told him I was going back to Canada and to pay for a ticket for us to return, he became very angry and wouldn't allow me to go back. I had no money, no friends, and no family that I could contact for help. When we were new in Canada and my time was taken up with taking David to the babysitter, Roger to school, and working, I sent a letter to my mother in Trinidad, and when she replied, he opened my mail, read it, and he gave it to me and said that when I write to my mother, I must give him the letter to read before I mail it. At that request, I didn't write to my mother again, for I knew if I wrote to my mother, and she responded, and he got the letter before I do, I was in for a beating. I thought about all the things I had bought, my clothes, my first pair of tall black leather winter boots that

I liked. My beautiful furniture in the apartment, all my personal belonging, everything that I had acquired.

He didn't allow me to return to Montreal and close out the apartment, or to let my job or our landlord know that we weren't coming back. I wasn't able to communicate with them. I also didn't know what would happen to my belongings. To this day I don't know; I was forced to abandon them.

I was settled in Canada and was uprooted, held hostage, and I couldn't do anything about the decision. It was very painful, and I submitted to the loss. I didn't walk away from it, but it was taken away from me. It was lost forever, never to be returned, and I never returned back to Canada. That was forty-nine years ago. In Cambridge, I enrolled Roger in school, and I found a babysitter for David and a job working at a ping-pong table tennis company on Third Avenue. We stayed in Cambridge for six months, and after the six months, he rented a three-bedroom duplex apartment on Cedar Street in Roxbury. We lived across from a school, the Nathan Hale school. Roger was seven, and David two years old. I registered Roger in school, and David stayed at home, and I didn't go back to work. I took care of Roger and David and became a housewife. After we moved to Roxbury, I found out that I was pregnant with my fourth child.

I had always desired to have a daughter, and when I was pregnant, I knew it was a baby girl. I had three boys and was excited I was having a girl. There wasn't ultrasound in those days, but I knew without a doubt, I was pregnant with a girl child. The time was coming closer for her to be born, and at six months pregnant, I went shopping, and I bought the crib and all the clothes in pink for a baby girl. I followed up with my maternity visits, every two weeks then once a week. One morning, I got up, fixed breakfast for the family, and Donald went off to work, and the boys to school. The night before, my water broke and I called the hospital. I had no pain, and I was told to come for a doctor's visit at the hospital the next day. After breakfast and everyone left, I called a taxi to take me to the hospital, and I waited for half an hour, and the taxi didn't show up. I left the house and walked to the main road, and I got a taxi to take me to Beth Israel Hospital. When I arrived, I went to the front desk and told the receptionist that I am here for a checkup and what happened the night before.

The hospital attendant brought a wheelchair for me, and I was taken to the elevator and to the labor and delivery room where I was examined. The baby was in the position ready to come. (I had no pain.) The nurse went through the procedure for the delivery and induce the labor. The anesthetic technician arrived and gave me an epidural anesthesia, and four hours later, I give birth to a baby girl, a daughter. I had left home that morning at 10:00 a.m., and the baby was born at 2:00 p.m. that afternoon. Her dad was at work and didn't know that I had given birth. When he came home that evening, he received a call from one of the nurses who told him I was in the hospital and had given birth to a baby girl. That was the easiest delivery I had compared to my previous pregnancies. And he came to the hospital, overjoyed with a vase of flowers and saw his daughter, and he named her, Debra. The next day, I was released, and he came again and took me home. I started crying after a couple weeks and couldn't understand why. I had experience a normal delivery and given birth to a healthy child, and I found out from my doctor that I was experiencing postpartum depression, but it lasted for a couple months with the new baby on board and the responsibility of the home, it became very challenging.

Roger attended school across the street and I found a babysitter for David. I took Debra in the stroller every day for walks and enjoyed spending time with her. She is a blessing to me from God. I did the cleaning and cooking and prepared dinner for the family, and I put the kids to bed at night time.

I wasn't allowed to do anything outside the house. Donald purchased my clothes, curtains for the home, the furniture, and whatever was needed in the home, and he chose the friends I should talk to.

From left to right: Grace, Debra, Roger, David

Meeting Dad

The first time I saw my father, I was four years old. I was playing in the yard with the other children. I was given a piece of chewing gum, and I chewed and swallowed. One of the kids asked me, "Where is the gum?" I said I swallowed it, and they started teasing me. "You will die," they said. I didn't know what death means, but to me it sound serious, and whatever death was, I didn't want it to happen to me, so I started crying. At the same time, a man walked into the yard and saw me crying and asked, "Why are you crying?"

"I swallowed chewing gum, and I am going to die, and I don't want to die."

He said to me, "You're not going to die," and I stopped crying. That man was my father. My father lived in Enterprise, Chaguanas, and the woman he lived with took me three times to spend a weekend with them. I heard them arguing, and I was afraid that it might be because of me being there, so I hid behind the sofa. In my childlike mind, I assumed that if I hide, I will not be a bother to them, and they will not send me away, and I will be invited back again. I heard them calling, "Joyce, Joyce," but I didn't answer.

I pretended I didn't hear them calling, and they kept searching. Eventually they pulled the sofa out and found me behind it crouched in a fetal position. They took me out and asked why was I behind the sofa, and I told them what I thought. Another time I went to spend the weekend, and this time I didn't hide when I heard the argument because I knew it wasn't my fault. One weekend before she took me back to my grandmother, she bought me new clothes, shoes, dress, and socks. Then she stopped coming and I never heard from her again. Questions I asked myself, "Why didn't she come or say that she couldn't come for me again?" I didn't understand, but there was no one to talk too about it, so I just internalized it, and after a while let it go. This was the second time I saw my dad after the chewing gum incident, and I did not seen him again for a long time. One day, as I was standing at the bus stop waiting for the bus, he drove up and stopped. (He drove a taxi.) He asked to take me home or wherever I was going, but I was very angry with him, and I said to him, "I don't need a ride from you. I have money to take the bus," and I didn't go with him, and he drove off. The next time I saw my dad, it was in Brooklyn, New York.

In 1970, when I was living in Cambridge, Massachusetts, Donald and I and our children went to visit my cousin, Janet, who lived in Brooklyn. She told me that she saw my father in Brooklyn, and he is married. I asked her if she knew his phone number. She said yes, and she gave it to me. I called the number, and he answered. I said hello.

He said, "Who is this?"

I said, "Your daughter."

There was a silence at the end of the line. "Where are you?"

"I'm in Brooklyn with my family, visiting Janet. I would like to see you."

And he gave me the address. I was married and had two children. My husband and I went over, and when he saw me, he couldn't believe it, but he was happy to see us. He had not told his wife, Louise, that he had a daughter. I met Louise for the first time, and she met me, the daughter that she hadn't known about with her children and husband. She was very surprised. We visited for a while, then we went back to Cambridge.

It wasn't until seven years later we met again and by that time my husband and I were divorced.

I was no longer angry with my dad and had acquired a love for him, and I called him daddy. He has apologized to me for not being there in my childhood, and he has also received redemption. We communicated regularly, and my children called him granddaddy when we visited. Louise, my stepmother, accepted me as her daughter and introduced me to her friends and neighbors as her daughter, and the kids call her Grandma Louise. Several times they came to Boston to visit us and stayed for the week. Dad moved from Brooklyn and went to live in Charlotte, North Carolina. I spent several Christmases in North Carolina visiting, and at times it felt like my second home. In 2007, my dad became sick and was in and out of the hospital. His grandchildren and I visited him a couple times in the hospital.

On March 24, 2009, he passed away. Louise called me, and I went to Charlotte. Together we went to the funeral home as mother and daughter, made preparations for his burial, and notified family and friends.

My dad and stepmother, Louise

Battered

Whenever we were invited to a party, I was not allowed to dance with anyone. I was to sit while he danced with anyone he wanted to dance with. If anyone were to ask me to dance, I was not allowed to dance with that person, and if I did, the beating started when we got home. One of our neighbors invited us to a Christmas party. He was dancing and enjoying himself. The neighbor needed ice and asked if he would go over to our apartment next door and get some ice. When he left to get the ice, I was sitting, but when he came back with the ice, I was dancing. He gave the ice to the neighbor and grabbed me and said it's time to leave, and he took me down to the basement, and the beating started. When we were out in public with the children, and a male person looked me. "Why is that man looking at you?" I didn't see the man, and I wasn't looking at anyone. I was enjoying the outdoors with my children, and when we got home, the beating started.

Almost every weekend, there was a beating. Before he came home in the evenings from work, I would fear an attack, and the beating started. I was beaten for almost anything which I didn't do. The beating became like a habit, and I began expecting it. Beat me and get over with it. I was aware of what was happening, but I had no control of it. This was the kind of life that I was living. I became addicted to the beatings. but the beating was like a drug someone was giving to me, and I was like a prisoner held against my will. Many times I went to the St. Elizabeth Hospital and other hospitals in the Boston area and in the emergency centers. There were times I was kept overnight and sent home the next morning. I was a regular visitor to the hospitals. When the nurses asked me what had happened, I lied, and I said I fell down the stairs. I didn't want my children to be without a father's presence in the home, and if I told them he did it, the law would have taken him away.

He didn't hurt the children physically, but they were there to see it. He adored his daughter. She could do no wrong. She was daddy's little girl that he loved. When I was a child, I didn't have my father around me. I saw him three times in my childhood, and then as an adult, I wanted to have a complete family unit for my children. What kept me holding on was the hope that one day, my children would be on their own and could take care of themselves. One day, I cleaned the apartment, cooked the food, and the children were taken care of, and when he came home, he went upstairs, and as he was coming back downstairs, he took the trash bin and threw the trash down the stairs, and he said, "You think you're Jesus Christ, you're so goody-goody!" I went to the stairs, picked up the trash, and swept the stairs. There were times when I left the apartment, and the children were sleeping after the beatings and walked the streets of Roxbury at two in the morning (it was by the grace of God, someone didn't hurt me) thinking, "What should I do?" And when I went back into the house, he was asleep.

I made a decision to leave him, and I called a hotel and made a room reservation, and I took the children with me. I needed to get away from the chaos. We were there for a couple of days, and the kids started whining, "Mommy, where's daddy? I want daddy." I told them that if I allowed them to call daddy, don't tell him where we were, but they told him. I called the number, gave them the phone, and they talked to him and then hung up. A couple hours after, there was a knock on the door, and I thought it was the hotel maid, and I opened the door, and there stood daddy at the door. He took the children, and we went back home. Things in the home was quiet for a while, and I went on with life. But suddenly a change occurred, and the beating started again. My head was swollen, and my body bruised all over. I didn't want to live, and I cried out to God. I said, "God, if this is life, I don't want to live. Take me." (At the time, I didn't know God doesn't take life he gives life.) And within me, I sensed a peace, and I heard, "It doesn't have to be this way." At that moment, I felt a surge of strength within me and knew what to do.

My cousin Janet lived in Brooklyn. I didn't want to bother her and her husband with my problem, but I came to the realization that it wasn't only my problem. We were family, and I wasn't ashamed to ask for help. I knew if I stayed in the marriage, I won't live to see my children as adults. I called and asked her if the kids and I could come and stay a while with them. She asked her husband, and they both agreed for the kids and I to come and stay with them in Brooklyn, New York. The next day, I prepared breakfast for Donald and the children. He went off to work and the children to school. When they left, I packed clothes for the children and me in a suitcase, then I got a ride from one of my neighbors to the Greyhound bus station in Boston. I went into the bus station and rented a locker and put the suitcase in the locker and went back home. When the kids came home from school, I fed them and told them that we are going to Brooklyn to visit Aunt Janet. I called a taxi, and we went to the Greyhound bus station. We boarded the bus and headed for Brooklyn, New York. I wasn't allowed to take care of anything in the house other than cooking, washing, cleaning, and my children.

I never gave any thought that Donald would recognize my cousin's phone number on the phone bill. He didn't called the number, but he discovered that's where I went. We were there for a month, and I enrolled Roger and David in school and had planned to get an apartment. One evening while we were having dinner, the doorbell rang, my cousin pressed the buzzer, and Donald walked in. He grabbed the children and took them to his car and headed for Boston. I went to the family children services in Brooklyn and made a report and was told that it will take months before I have a hearing. I then went to the police station in Brooklyn and filed a report against him for kidnapping the children. Neither of us had legal custody, so it wasn't kidnapping. He was their father, and I was told that they were in Boston and out of their jurisdiction. My children, whom I was protecting, were taken from me and no longer with me, and I didn't know what to do.

I stayed in Brooklyn for a couple months and called them by phone every day. One day when I called they were crying and my mother's instinct told me that things weren't right and that my children weren't being taken care of. My neighbor, Bertha, lived in the apartment next door; she would visit her mother in Georgia in the summer for months and at that time that's where she was. I called her and asked her if I could stay in her apartment for a while, and she agreed. I took the Greyhound bus headed for Boston and stayed in her apartment, and the next day, when Donald left for work, I went next door and saw my children. The apartment was mess. Clothes weren't washed and were thrown all together into a pile. I told them that I was in Boston, and I am staying over at Ms. Bertha's apartment. I cooked and cleaned up the apartment before he came home from work, and then I went back over to Bertha's apartment. He knew that I was in the neighborhood, but I didn't care. He didn't bother me. Every day I went over, and I took care of my children. I fed them, cleaned the apartment, and I cooked enough food for Donald and the children and went back to my neighbor's apartment.

I was referred by a friend to legal aid services, and I called them up and made an appointment to see a lawyer, and I was given a day and a time to meet with the lawyer. I met with the lawyer, and I told him about the beatings and asked to see a judge for a restraining order. He made an appointment, and I went to court with the lawyer. We went before a judge, and I told the judge about the beatings, and I was given the restraining order. I went to the store after and bought a lock for the apartment door. I went home, and I changed the lock (with help), and that evening when Donald came home from work, I was in the apartment. Donald turned his keys in the front door, but it didn't work. Then he realized the lock was changed, and he kicked the door in. I ran out the back door and went to a neighbor's apartment and called the police. When I saw the police cars drove up, I went back to the apartment, and I showed them the restraining order, and they told him he had to leave the apartment right away. They allowed him to take some of his things and come back for the balance of things another day, but before he came back, he needed to have a police officer escorting him to the apartment.

The next day, he was escorted to the apartment, and he took the balance of his things. He was out of the apartment, and I never let him into it again. It was a nasty scene, but I had to do it. "Free. I am free. Thank God, whom Jesus the son sets free is free indeed. I am free indeed." I was afraid that he would stalk me and try to hurt me, but he didn't. I called the legal aid services lawyer and filed for a divorce, and they gave me an appointment. I was given a date and time to see the judge, and Donald was served with the court papers. On the day for the court hearing, I went to court, but Donald didn't appear. The judge asked me if I want to changed my last name, and I said, "No, allow the children and me to stay in the apartment, and not have to be removed to a new surroundings," and he granted it. The divorce became final, and after six months, I was divorced. I filed for child support. I didn't want alimony, only support for my children, and it was granted. He was given visitation rights to have the children every other weekend and was not allowed to come into the apartment. I kept the name until the children were grown and on their own, and I changed back to my maiden name.

My children grew up and completed their education. Two got married and have children of their own. Two of them have established their own businesses, and the other is successfully employed. I am a grandmother of three, two boys, one married, and a granddaughter. After several years, Donald sent me a letter and apologized for how he had treated me and asked me to forgive him, and I forgave him. When two of our children got married, we were both invited to their weddings. We both represented our children at the ceremonies and Donald and I sat together on the front row at the church. The pictures were taken together with both parents and the bride and groom. There are times when Donald was given a birthday party by his children, and they included me in the celebration. Whenever Donald had a concern about one of the children, he reaches out to me for moral support. Donald has received redemption through the shed blood of Jesus Christ.

Divorced

I felt like a bird that was set free from its cage. After the divorce I was very happy and began to smile again. One day one of my children said to me, "Mom, if you didn't leave daddy, I would have run away." I had low self-esteem. I was timid and suffered with anxiety attacks. But I told myself I made it through the beatings and I would make it through this and overcome it. I looked so joyful and happy. People I knew before the divorce saw the change. The children continued to attend school, and I got a job working at McDonald's, mother's hours. Sometimes the children got home before me. When I came home from work, I cooked and we had dinner; I helped them with their homework and then sent them off to bed. I had my own home for the first time in my life and was enjoying it and my life with my children. Roger was fourteen, David nine, and Debra five years old. I was happy and we were happy together.

I took business courses at night school, applied for an administrative assistant job at a company in Boston, and got the job. My working hours changed and I was paid more. I bought a car. The kids were older and were able to manage doing things for themselves. Roger helped to take care of his brother and sister if I was late coming home from work. I enjoyed going to parties, and on weekends, there was always a party at one of my coworkers' homes on a Friday or Saturday night, and Roger would babysit. And there were times when I and my co-workers all got together and went disco dancing; that was my entertainment. Roger went off to college, and it was just David, Debra, and me at home. Paul, the nephew of a friend, came from Mississippi to visit his aunt and she gave him a welcome party, and I was invited to the party. We were introduced and we started talking and became friends. Paul was new to Boston, and I showed him around the city. We went to Quincy Market and sampled the food at Faneuil Hall, and we went to museums, whale watching, and other places.

We went out and had a wonderful time together; he liked Boston and he decided to stay. I enjoyed his company; we went on sightseeing trips to New York. We enjoyed spending time together. He left his aunt's home and moved in with me and we lived together for a year. He was on and off with jobs and couldn't find steady or permanent work, and eventually decided to go back to his hometown. He asked me to go with him, but David and Debra were attending school. I didn't want to interrupt their education and have them continue in a new school or state, and I didn't go with him. Paul left and went back to his hometown and I was heartbroken. I cared for him a lot, but I couldn't see myself making this big change in my children's lives, and I made the decision not to go with him.

Born Again

I was working at Keystone Life Insurance and one day on a lunch break I met a coworker, Brenda Turner. We discovered that we lived near each other. We exchanged phone numbers, and the following week, I called her. We met and had lunch together, and we became friends. We started talking about church. There was a hunger in our hearts for more of life, but we didn't know what it was. She didn't attend a church, neither did I. One day, we decided to find a church, and one Sunday morning we met and went to visit a church in her neighborhood where she lived. We didn't know the dress code, and we went like the saying, "Come just as you are." It was summertime and we both were wearing thin spaghetti-strap dresses. The church had a billboard in front that mentioned the name of Jesus. We went in the church and looked for a seat, and we sat down. The people were looking at us as if to say, "What are you doing here dressed like that?" They kept staring at us and didn't acknowledge that we were there.

We felt very uncomfortable, and I looked at Brenda, and she looked at me as if to say, "Let's get out of here," and we both got up and left. We sometimes teased each other and would say, "We are church hunting." We went to a couple of churches but didn't feel welcome. One Sunday morning we left the church and went to a seafood restaurant, and we felt more welcome there than at the churches we had visited. One day, Brenda told me that she found a church in Cambridge, St. Paul AME Church, and it's different than the ones we went to before. I was doubtful. I said to myself, "I will go and see what it's like, and if it's like the ones we went to before, I won't go back." She gave me the address of the church and the directions, and we planned to meet at the front of the church and then go in together. When I arrived, she was standing at the front of the church, and we went in together. It was different from the churches we went to before; I felt welcome. Brenda had visited before, and she like it. I attended a couple of times, and the pastor preached about salvation and asked the people who hadn't made a commitment for Christ to come to the front, and he prayed for them.

I sat and listened. I didn't respond, and I stopped going. Then one day Brenda called me and told me that St Paul's was having a revival service, and she invited me to come. At that time I didn't know what a revival service was; I had never heard of them before. She told me that the evangelist was from the Go Tell It Ministry from Detroit, Michigan, and was used by God in the gifts of the Spirit. In my heart, I got a warm feeling inside me that I must accept the invitation, but I didn't know what Brenda meant by being used in the gifts of the Spirit. I was at work, and I called my friend and next-door neighbor, Bertha, and told her what Brenda had told me, and that the meeting started at seven that night. It was a Monday, the first night of the revival. Bertha said she would go, and after work I went home and met her and we drove to Cambridge to the revival service. After the first night, I couldn't wait for the next night to go back again. I had settled in my heart to attend the two weeks' revival service.

On the third night of the revival, the evangelist, a woman, went and stood at the back of the church and said, "Bow your head and let the Holy Spirit speak to your heart and tell you where you are with Him."

I bowed my head, and I heard one foot in and one foot out, and I knew exactly what that meant. I said, "I'm not sure, and I heard, 'Come and be sure.'" I stood up and stepped out from where I was sitting and headed to the front of the church. There was a crowd of people standing up to the front of the church, and I joined them. The evangelist went back to the front of the church and stood on the platform, and she asked everyone to bow their heads and say the prayer after her. We all prayed, and after we prayed, we were taken to a room where we gave our names and were welcomed into the family of God. That was October 25, 1983. The revival lasted for fourteen straight days with a service every night at seven, and each midday the evangelist taught a Bible study class. I attended the night services and the midday Bible studies, taking time from my lunch hour at work to go. I was on a spiritual high after the revival, and my life was changed.

I was in a dark place in my life, and I believed God sent the evangelist to pull me out of darkness into His marvelous light. I was on a dead-end street going nowhere. I went to work, and I enjoyed my job. My children were happy, and I was enjoying life. I partied almost every weekend, but something wasn't right. I had a deep emptiness in my heart. There were times when I went home after work and sat outdoors on my stairs and asked myself, "What is life all about?" I wanted to know. I was happy with my material things, but something was missing, and I didn't know what it was. When Jesus came into my life, everything changed, the emptiness left and a peace that I never knew before filled my heart. When Jesus came into my life a new life began, and I was never the same old way again, and I never want to be that same old way again. The following year, in the spring, the grass and trees looked greener, and my surroundings looked brighter. I thought that everyone else was living this beautiful experience and I had just connected to it.

One Saturday I went to the Boston Farmers' market at Haymarket Square, an outdoor market located near the Boston Waterfront and Faneuil Hall in Boston's North End. The market is opened year 'round on Fridays and Saturdays from dawn to dusk and sells fresh produce from carts and stands that crowd the sidewalk against a market building filled with small butcher and other specialty food shops, that all open onto the sidewalk. It's like the market in Trinidad that my grandmother and I went to on Saturdays.

One day, I drove to the Haymarket and was looking for a parking space. When I went to the Haymarket before, I always found a parking space within five or ten minutes; someone pulls out and I pull into the space. That Saturday I sat in my car waiting for someone to pull out, but that didn't happen for a long while. Something told me to go to the supermarket instead to get what I wanted, but I was stubborn. I said to myself, "I always get a parking space, and this time I am going to get one." I waited and waited for about an hour, and I saw someone going toward their parked car. I was so happy, and I pulled into the space. But before I left the car, I thought to separate my keys from my money purse and put them into my other pocket, separate from my money, then I headed to the fruits and vegetables stands.

I picked up a bunch of bananas and asked for it to be weighed. Being told how much it cost, I reached into my coat pocket to get my money purse, but it wasn't there. I had been pickpocketed! The Haymarket is a very crowded place. It's like people are almost stuck to you rubbing against the crowd with no room between. I remembered that I had thought to go instead to the supermarket, and I did. I went home for some money and then went to the supermarket and bought my fruits and vegetables. This was also the first time I really heard clearly, saw, my inner guidance (which I would say is God's guidance) giving me such clear direction—to move my keys and to go to the supermarket instead of Haymarket—and from that moment, I began to give myself space to identify, listen to, and hear that inner guidance.

The revival experience also brought to me an awareness that there were others who needed to connect to the born-again experience but who weren't, and I began to seek ways for how I could help connect them. I attended St. Paul's AME Church and was an usher for one year. Before I went to St. Paul's, I had watched Believer's Voice of Victory Ministry and was a partner with the ministry, and I watched Ever-Increasing Faith Ministry before I was born again, but I didn't understood things about the Holy Spirit, and I didn't know God the Holy Spirit.

Whenever I watched the programs, I enjoyed the teachings. It brought to me a sense of goodness, love, and hope. I had a program scheduled, and every day I knew the time the Believer's Voice of Victory and Ever-Increasing Faith and Brother Hagin's the Word of Faith came on the television, and I tuned in to watch. Then cable was available for a small cost, and I had cable, and I could watch the program at different times. When I missed the morning program, I listened to it at night. I made watching the teaching of the word of God like my soap opera. The Believer's Voice of Victory Broadcast came on in the early mornings, at noon, and at night, and also Ever-Increasing Faith and Brother Hagin's the Word of Faith Ministry. I scheduled all my appointments and shopping around the times the programs came on, so I wouldn't miss the teachings, and I enjoyed watching and learning about what faith is. I learned, for example, that faith is the substance of things hoped for, the evidence of things not seen. This was different than what I heard when I lived in Trinidad; there wasn't teaching from the Bible there, but instead someone talking about the bible. I went to church every Sunday, sang the hymns, gave the offering, and went home, but in Trinidad I learned very little from the Bible.

The first year that I was born again, I had this experience; I couldn't sleep in my bedroom. I wasn't comfortable sleeping in my bedroom, and one night I took my sheets, a pillow, and a blanket, and I made a bed on the sofa of my living room and sleep there all night. I continued to sleep in the living room for about two weeks, and while I slept, I kept receiving this thought as guidance. "Go to your bedroom and get all the books on the shelves, take them down and throw them out into the trash bin." I thought to myself, "Those books cost money, and they are good books," but I obeyed. I bought some boxes and went to my bookshelves, and I put all the books that I had bought before I was born again into the boxes. I had a couple boxes filled with books, and I took them to the dumpster. But before I dumped them, I heard myself saying, "Give it to somebody. They might like them and read them." And again I was guided, "If they aren't good for you, why give it to someone else?" And I dumped the boxes of books into the bin and went back into my apartment. That night, I took my sheets, the pillow, and my blanket from the sofa, and I went to my bedroom, made up my bed, and I slept all night and continued to sleep and enjoyed sleeping again in my bedroom.

I loved reading, and I had bought and read books that were not of a spiritual nature but on a set of beliefs and rituals that claimed to get a person in a right relationship with God (these the ones I threw away). I began to research and read books that were of a spiritual nature, and I saw the difference. I saw that I didn't have to go through rituals to have a relationship with God. I needed only to acknowledge what the Bible said is true, accept His word, and believe. I bought books from the ministries that I listened to weekly and from the church bookstore (at Faith Fellowship Ministry). Before I'd leave church, I'd visit the bookstore and buy five or more mini-books, and when I went home I read every one of them. Sometimes it was two in the morning before I went to bed.

Ghana Mission

After being born again I became an usher at St. Paul's. I met there Andrea Thomas who also was born again at the revival and we became friends. Although we went to the Sunday service and Wednesday Bible study, we both hungered for more of the Word of God teaching. But the St. Paul's pastor's teaching was more about the born-again experience. Andrea listened to a Bible teaching that was broadcast weekly from Faith Fellowship Ministry in Winchester, Massachusetts, and she invited me to go with her to visit their church. We went to the 8:00 a.m. service at St. Paul's and then drove to Faith Fellowship for the 11:00 a.m. service., We did this for a couple of months.

I also listened to Brother Hagin's teaching on the radio. One day he announced a two-weeks' night revival in Winter Haven, Florida. I mentioned it to Andrea and we decided to go. We drove from Boston to Winter Haven and stayed for one week. Every night we went to the meetings and listened to the Word of God being taught. We were new believers and in our spirit of joy we laughed and worshiped and praised the Lord together.

The experience was new to us, and we enjoyed being in the presence of the Lord. After the seventh day of the revival, we headed back to Boston, stopping only for gas. When we came back to Boston, we made the decision to attend one church service. I made an appointment with the pastor, and I told him I was leaving. Andrea and I left St. Paul's in 1984 and joined Faith Fellowship Ministry. There we attended church and completed their two years' Victory Bible School Training program. We graduated in 1988.

Andrea then left Massachusetts and moved to another state, but we kept in contact. Twelve years later, in 2000, I enrolled in their Student's Advanced Leadership training, graduating the same year. Before graduation, the dean of the school planned a mission trip for the class to visit Accra, Ghana, in West Africa. I chose to go and traveled with the team of Bible students. We had completed a third-year course in theology. We flew from Logan Airport, Boston, to Heathrow Airport, London, where we waited for several hours before boarding the flight to Ghana.

The flight scheduled from Boston was eleven and a half hours. I had travel to Japan on a fourteen-hour trip and was prepared for the trip. When we arrived in Accra, Ghana, we were met at the airport by the directors of the organization, Reverend Ray and Joycelyn who invited us to come and help with the work that they were doing in Ghana, Africa. We collected our luggage. There were two vans waiting to take us to the hotel, and when we arrived that night, we were given the program with an itemized listing of the places that we would visit, wake up, and travel time. The trip included visiting two schools in Dodowa. We were given a room for two, and we went to bed after midnight. The next morning, we had an early breakfast, and we were off to one of the schools in Dodowa. We visited and distributed school supplies to each classroom, and we met with the children. They welcomed us in songs as we sang with them. They taught us new songs, and we taught them the songs we knew. The next day, we visited another school in the Dodowa village. They wore uniforms just like I did in Trinidad in my childhood. They were lined up in the schoolyard and walked behind each other into their classrooms.

When I saw the children, it was like living and experiencing my childhood all over again. They reminded me of the times I stood in the schoolyard and walked into my classroom in my school days. I looked at the children, and I started to cry. The children were the same age as I when I attended school in Trinidad and Tobago. I remembered the difficult and lonely times of my childhood, and I asked myself, "Why am I crying?" I didn't understand at the time my genes were connected to theirs through our ancestors, and I didn't know about my ancestors and my genes, and that I was related to Ghana through my ancestors and in the company of my tribes. I felt connected to them; that experience was nineteen years ago. The next day, we went to Tamale. We had a ten-hours bus ride from Accra to Tamale village. Joycelyn cooked and packed a basket with food and juice for everyone. (She is a Trinidadian, and it was good to see her.) The bus ride didn't allow time to stop and buy food. The only time we stopped was to stretch our legs and use the restroom, which was rare. There wasn't a restroom but an open booth stall, and after using it, we poured water over the urine to wash the concrete floor. When we went to Tamale, we stayed in a motel. The room was comfortable, and the food was good. I had a headache and was exhausted. We ate, and I went to bed. The next morning, we got up early and took the bus to Tamale village. (I was told that the Sahara wasn't too far away.)

The village was filled with small mud huts. The red dirt was so beautiful, and the people of the village were waiting for us. The people were told by the directors that a medical team would be coming and for the chief of the village to gather the people in an open space. A medical team of doctors, nurses and assistants had come from Accra with medical supplies for the people in Tamale village; they set up their station and we joined them. We met the chief and his assistants. The people began coming. Many were sick with different diseases and were treated. The children, pregnant woman, and elderly stood in a line, while the team prayed for those with different health needs. The village water pipeline was shut off because they couldn't afford to pay the water bill, and there wasn't a water supply in the village. The team donated money for the water supply to be turned on. We were invited into the chief's hut, and we took pictures with the chief and his assistant in the village yard. All of the people in the whole village were treated; there was a large turnout of people. We stayed in the village the whole day, and at the end of the day, we headed back to the town. We had dinner at the motel inn, and after dinner we stayed up, and we sat around and talked about the day's activities.

The next morning, we boarded the bus and headed back to Accra. On the sixth day, the night before we left, Joycelyn made dinner for us with different selections, maakye, kele wele (spicy fried plantain), Omo tuo (rice balls), Fufo (cassava), and many other dishes. The day of travel, Reverend Ray and Joycelyn took us to the airport, and we boarded the plane. We had a six-and-half-hour flight, and we arrived at Heathrow airport in England in the morning. We had a long layover; the departure flight to Boston wasn't leaving Heathrow airport until that evening. The dean suggested that we take the train to the downtown, and we agreed. We went downtown and took the double-decker bus to a cafe and had breakfast. We visited the Buckingham Palace gate and saw the changing of the guards. As we stood at the gate suddenly the guards came out and changed places. We took a team picture with the guards in the background, then we took the train back to the airport and checked our flight departure time. There was a four-hour delay. We waited with the other travelers while some members of the team spread out on benches as we waited.

Then it was time to board our flight for Boston. The flight arrived in Logan Airport after seven hours and we were connected with family members and friends waiting to pick us up. We hugged and promised to see each other at church on Sunday, said our goodbyes, and then we left and went home.

Haiti Mission,
"Life on the Mission Field"

Before I went to Ghana in 2000, I went in 1992 to Leogane, Haiti, for six months as a missionary. The directors were George and Jeanne De Tellis, of New Mission Christian Organization, based in Miami. I was working at University Hospital in Boston. At that time, Haiti was in a crisis. New Mission had a relationship with Faith Fellowship Ministry, where I was a member, and they came one Sunday and gave a presentation. I took a brochure and in it was an invitation to a morning breakfast given by the mission directors, and I signed up to attend. At the breakfast they talked about their work in Haiti and the need for missionaries to serve. I felt a quickening in my heart to respond to the need. I was employed and had a beautiful apartment. My children were on their own and I was living single, but I wanted to do something to help humanity in some way in service. I prayed for direction, whether I am to respond or not, but I had this deep desire to go. When I doubted, a sadness came over me, and when I ignored the doubt, I had peace, and I followed peace.

I shared my desire to serve on the mission with others, and was told that there was a joy on my face when I spoke about going. I had such peace that I should go that I made the decision to go to Haiti as a missionary. I applied to the New Mission directors and was accepted. They sent me an application to fill out and return with a recommendation from my pastor. I filled out the form, and I went to my pastor and told him what my plans were, and that I needed a recommendation, which I received with his permission, and I sent in the form. I was accepted and given several departure dates and times for travel to Haiti. I went to work, and I told my supervisor that I am going to Haiti as a missionary, and I gave her my two weeks' notice. On the day I left the job, I received my salary, vacation pay that I had acquired, and severance pay. It also happened they were closing an employee investment account and refunding money, and mine was returned to me. I said goodbye to my coworkers and left the job.

I called American Airlines and booked my flight to Port-au-Prince. My commitment was for six months, and I didn't have storage for my car. I had this bright idea to sell my car, which I did, and the money went toward my expenses. I went to my rental home owner and told her that I was going to Haiti on a mission trip for six months, and I will pay her for the six months, and when I come back from Haiti, I will continue to pay the rent, and she agreed. I had my utilities disconnected. My departure day and time arrived. A friend drove me to Logan Airport and I was on my way to Haiti. At that time America Airlines flights weren't going to Haiti because of an uprising there. But they arranged for my ticket to be honored by the Haitian airline. I flew to Miami, transferred, and when I arrived at the airport in Port-au-Prince, went through customs and immigration checkpoints with the other travelers and headed to baggage section.

The passengers who traveled on the same flight with me picked up their luggage and left, but mine wasn't there. I stood at the counter and was told that my luggage hadn't arrived. I was given a receipt and was told to come back the next day, that maybe it was delayed. The director of the mission met me at the airport in Port-au-Prince and we drove to the mission compound in Leogane, about 26 miles, an hour's drive. We arrived about 8:00 p.m. I was shown my quarters where I put away what I had, and then went to the dining area. I had a light snack that was kept warm for me. I ate, said good night to everyone and went to my quarters and went to bed. That night I heard a sound like rain falling heavily. In the morning when I awoke and I went for breakfast, I said to one of the missionaries, "It rained all night heavily, but the ground is dry." And I couldn't understand why that happened. She said, "It must be the waves of the ocean you heard splashing on the shore." And when I looked out, I saw the ocean. It was about a five-minute walk from the mission compound, and that's what I heard that night. The next day I went with one of the permanent missionaries to the school in Leogane village.

We were greeted by the children and we gave out school supplies. I didn't have extra clothes, only the clothes that I wore to travel and my pocket book, but the director gave me some of her clothes to wear. It was midweek, and she went to Port-au-Prince to purchase food and supplies for the mission school feeding program and for the missionaries. She went to the airport and checked on my luggage before returning to the mission compound, but it wasn't there. The other missionaries suggested that maybe it was lost, and I would never get my luggage, but I wasn't concerned. I believed that I was sent to Haiti to help people in need. When I prayed about going, I had a peace that it was going to be all right, and I said to them, "I will get my luggage, even if an angel has to bring it." A week later the director again going to Port-au-Prince for supplies said she would stop once more at the airport to check for my luggage, but that if it couldn't be found, she would consider it lost and that would be her final trip to the airport.

She went to the airport luggage claims department to inquire about my luggage and was told that it wasn't there. She went looking into the empty rooms around and was about to leave, and she said something told her to go back and look into another room, and there was my suitcase, broken, tucked in the corner of the room. I had given her a description of it, and it looked like mine. She picked it up carefully and brought it to the mission compound, and when I saw it, I was so happy. I took it from her, and everything I packed was there. Nothing was missing, and after I emptied it I threw the broken case into the trash. I came to realize that while I had booked a direct flight to Haiti, it wasn't a direct flight. And when I changed planes in Miami, I should have brought my case with me. Instead it stayed in Miami.

The missionaries were short-term or long-term, short being the two weeks or so that some church groups came for. Because I committed to six months I was long-term. Long-term missionaries took turns by the month being responsible for breakfast and dinner, and I was put on duty one week after I arrived.

Breakfast was served at 7:00, before the missionaries headed to their assigned duties, and I had to be in the kitchen by 5:00. The kitchen/dining room was a separate building from the living quarters and about a five-minute walk away. The first morning I got up, it was dark, and I didn't like the pitch darkness. I took the flashlight, and breathing fast, I headed to the kitchen and dining building in the back of the compound. I made it into the kitchen, turned on the light, washed my hands, and started to scramble dozens of eggs, toast several loaves of bread, prepare fruit, fry bacon, and make coffee. I looked at the clock hanging on the wall; it was almost time for the missionary team to arrive at the dining table. I put the large plate of toast, the eggs, bacon, fruits, and coffee on the table as they opened the dining room door and sat down at the table. Wow! I made it! I did.

The next morning, I was calmer. I had successfully completed making breakfast for a large group. I woke up, dressed, picked up my flashlight, and headed for the kitchen for my second day. As I was walking toward the building on the dirt road, I saw a couple of cows laying across the road. I panicked. "What must I do to drive them away?" And as I started walking slowly toward them and praying under my breath, they suddenly got up and walked away. I ran to the kitchen as fast as I could, opened the door, ran inside and started to prepare breakfast, thinking to myself, "If I ever see a snake in my pathway, I am done making breakfast," but I didn't.

I was given the menu for the week, everything needed already there. And I didn't mind making dinner in the evening. The days were bright and sunny. I also didn't have to clean up; local Haitian women were hired to clean the kitchen so that they could have an income to feed their children, and many of them were single mothers. Then I completed my first cooking assignment and I looked forward to sitting at the dining table and just having breakfast and not having to cook again until my next turn.

Dinner was served at five in the evening. After dinner the missionaries had free time to read, go for walks on the beach, or go swimming. We worked Monday through Friday. On weekends the schools were closed, workers had the weekend off, and the missionaries had free time to visit the city or write letters to family and friends at home.

Monday evenings were the highlight of the week for the missionaries. The directors went to Port-au-Prince for supplies and also picked up the mail, and we all hoped for news from home. Electricity for the mission compound was provided by a generator. The lights was turned on in the morning and turned off at nine at night; some of the missionaries went to bed early, others stayed up, and on moonlit nights the whole compound was lit up like it was daytime.

When there was no moonlight it was very, very dark, and I could see the stars in the sky twinkling just as I did in my childhood in Trinidad. I enjoyed living and serving on the mission field in Haiti. The directors were very generous with the local men and women; they lived to serve the Haitian people. They had pastored a church in the US, but out of a deep desire to help the Haitian people they relocated to Haiti and established New Missions in Leogane.

I cooked breakfast and dinner for the missionaries for three of my six months' commitment, alternating a month on and a month off. But my regular assignment for the full six months was to the school feeding program, and in that role I managed that kitchen and supervised the kitchen workers. I scheduled the weekly menu and got food and supplies daily from the program's warehouse. Every Monday through Friday morning at 7:00 I met with the cooks and kitchen workers. We got the food to be cooked that day and brought it to the school kitchen where it was prepared and cooked on six gas stoves in six 35-40 gallon iron pots (chodye), holding enough to serve 3,200 students every day. (Now, 27 years later, as part of its education mission, New Missions of Haiti serves about ten thousand students per school day (newmissions.org).) The children's favorite food were the rice and beans (dire and pwa). On Friday, the workers were paid, and I collected their salary from the mission accountant and paid the kitchen workers, the cooks, and the food distributors.

There were fifty-four villages, and the students that attended the schools came from the villages where they lived and were fed in the school feeding program. The directors of the mission built the schools in the villages where the children lived. In 1992 there were seven kindergartens, eleven primary schools, and a high school in the villages, a total of eighty-one classes and ninety-eight teachers. Also a medical clinic open five days weekly and missionary nurses available twenty-four hours, seven days a week for emergencies.

The mission directors hired a total of 180 local Haitian employees, including the cooks for the school feeding program, the school teachers, and other workers on the mission compound. Local women cooked the food for the school feeding program in the kitchen compound and the men carried the food in buckets on a wheelbarrow and distributed and served it in the village schools' eating centers. There were thirty-eight paid local school kitchen workers, including the cooks and men who distributed the food to the eating centers.

They hired teachers for the school feeding program and trained them to be pastors in pastoral care to care for the children. On Sundays, the school centers were used as the village church, and the teachers who taught the children in the school feeding program were the pastors who also taught the school children on Sundays. The children who attended the school on weekdays in the school program, also attended church services on Sundays. Some of the children came with their parents and others came alone. The children who didn't attend the school's program were welcome to attend the church services on Sundays. The directors of New Mission built their first church in BordMer village near the mission compound. It was open on Friday nights, including a revival service once a month, to all the local villagers. Long-term missionaries were assigned to villages to oversee Bible study groups on Wednesday evenings and to get there they could either walk or ride one of the bicycles that were available. Being a long-termer, I liked taking a bicycle.

On Sundays we attended church services. The directors drove to one of the village churches to preach the word and we missionaries went with them. We also had a service on Fridays after dinner. On those evenings one of the missionaries was chosen to speak and teach to all of us the word of God.

While I was there, several short-term missionary teams came from various churches in the US and other parts of the world to serve. We prepared the short-team mission quarters for them and planned the activities and outreach to the different villages that the teams would visit. The director would pick them up at the airport and take them to their quarters, and a late dinner was prepared for them.

The next morning they were shown the mission and taken to the villages. Those with skills to build and fix things formed a work team, with the others helping. After dinner at night, they were taken to the village in Ti Brache for a revival service, where they both met the people and preached the word of God. For their part, the people enjoyed having visitors. The people came and the pastor preached.

There were other times when the directors and the short-term mission team went to Ti Riviere village and the other villages with the food truck and gave out rice. We planned many activities for the short-term mission teams that came while I was there. In my fifth month a pastor from Dorchester, Massachusetts, came with his church members on a short-term mission visit for two weeks.

I lived in Cambridge at the time and was excited to see a team from Massachusetts. The activities were scheduled for the team to visit the villages and both meet the people and work. Before the team left, the pastor invited me to visit his church in Dorchester, and he gave me the address. When my six months were finished, I was ready to return home. I enjoyed the time that I spent on the mission field. I saw the many ways that the people's needs were taken care of and the souls that were saved. I had fulfilled my desire and made a difference and enjoyed it!

Abortion

It felt good and was good to arrive back home in Cambridge, but I also missed Haiti, the people, the place, even the short-term missionary visitors. When I left I was asked to come back, but that wasn't in God's plan. Haiti is a different lifestyle and I had to re-adjust my life again to my environment and our fast-paced American life. I went to visit the pastor's church in Dorchester on a Sunday morning. I wanted to surprise him. When I entered the church he was at the pulpit speaking to his congregation, and as I walked in, he looked up. He was surprised to see me. He introduced me after to his wife and children, and we talked for a while. He told me that he had started a ministry, A Woman's Concern, a free pregnancy testing center, to help women who were considering abortion to choose life for their unborn baby. He said that when we met in Haiti, he *felt* that I might be the person to work with him in establishing a center where women could come and get help.

I wasn't yet employed and agreed to take the assignment. It was going to be part-time. We made an appointment to meet at his office and discussed the details of the assignment. We put together a pamphlet, got a phone and an advertisement in the yellow pages, and researched referral resources. He rented space on Dorchester Avenue, Boston, and the center was opened to the public. He was the president, and I was the director. I worked at the center five days a week part-time. I recruited volunteers, distributed our pamphlets to local churches, and spoke to church groups. One day in one our meetings he asked me, "Have you ever had an abortion?" And I said no. But when I left the center that day and was driving home, all of a sudden I was flooded with the memory of two abortions I had as a teenager, both the result of rapes. I had buried the memories, and I broke down crying.

The next day when I went back to the center, I told him about my discovery. It was his question that made me remember; I had blocked conscious memory of the assaults and abortions for over thirty years, but they were not forgotten. I didn't deny the memory. I took hold of the memories and accepted them, and I also believed that I will give an account for my actions (2 Corinthians 5:10, NLT). There have been times when I dreamt of children every night over and over, and some nights I would stay up longer at night before I went to bed because the dreams kept recurring. Then one night they stopped. I didn't have those dreams again and I forgot about them. When I looked back to the past, I remembered crying every night, and I couldn't understand why I cried and cried at night when I went to bed, and my pillow would be soaking wet with tears in the morning. When I awoke the next morning, I didn't know why, and after many years I stopped crying at night; and I had buried all of it.

One night I went to bed and had a different dream (this was many years after the crying). I dreamt that there were two babies looking at me. I reached out my hands to them and they crawled towards me and I hugged them. One of them was a little bit older than the other one, and in my dream, they seemed to be alone with each other, and I had this premonition that they were the babies that I had aborted as a teenager, and that they weren't connected to a family. I put my arms around them and brought them close to me, and I gave them names when I awoke. I acknowledged them as part of my family, and such peace came over me, and I looked forward to meeting them in heaven in the future. God forgives (Psalms 103:12, KJV). As far as the east is from the west, so far had he removed my transgressions from me.

Patterns

When I lived with my grandmother, she didn't have a home of her own. We lived at one of her son's or daughter's home. I felt very unstable as a child and when I became an adult I had the same experiences. I didn't stay on a job for more than a year or two; the longest time was five years. The same thing happened also with residency. When I raised my children, I lived for eighteen years in an apartment, but when they were grown and on their own, I moved every few years. I began to see a pattern of how my childhood life was shaping my adult life. I had never been hugged as a child. I couldn't receive hugs or compliments. But for my cousin Janet, hugs were easy for her to give and receive. I'd ask myself, "How does she do that?" I went to a church as an adult and the pastor's wife came to greet me; she hugged me and I drew back away from her as if saying, "Don't touch me!" At that time, I wasn't aware of how much pain and insecurity I was carrying that had been with me from childhood.

As I am writing my memoir, I felt the hurt and pain, how she might have felt when I drew back from her, and I began to feel sad and cried. The tears began to flow from my eyes as I asked her to forgive me. In time past, I blocked hurt feelings I didn't want to feel the hurt. Now I no longer block hurt feelings. I receive it, and I let it go. (Hurtful memories bring hurt feelings, and happy memories bring happy feelings.) I lived with three foster relatives, my grandmother and aunts. I was divorced from my first husband and remarried again. I feel safe in my marriage. When I began to better understand my childhood experiences, the cycles stopped. I saw in my adult life the same patterns that had governed my early life.

Nothing in my life was stable. And now as an adult I was caught in and reliving the same instability. I was unable to stay in jobs or live in an apartment or home for more than a short time or keep friends. I was a child with an unstable upbringing and had feelings of insecurity and abandonment, of being unloved, fearful, damaged, and anxious. I was an impoverished person.

As an adult, I had not known why I was having such a difficult life. Even though I fought many obstacles and overcame many difficulties by perseverance and will power, life was difficult and hard. I was fighting with life all the time as I dealt with anxieties and fears that tracked me and overwhelmed me about losing things that I had acquired, loneliness, and not being accepted.

I was living the experiences as an adult that I lived as a child with my aunts and grandmother. Praise God! Light has shone in darkness, and I am no longer trapped by my past experiences. When Jesus came into my life, a new life begins, and I am no longer the same fearful, alone, insecure person. I give hugs and I like to be hugged!

Grace,
My Beginnings Didn't
Dictate My Future!

J oyce to Grace. For all my life I had been called Joyce. In kindergarten, through my school years, in Trinidad, and into adulthood. In 1967, as a citizen of Trinidad, I applied for a passport. My Trinidad ID card had the name Joyce on it, and with it I got my passport with my four-year-old son, Roger, also on it, and we both traveled on the same passport to Canada. In Canada I obtained immigration status. My first marriage was in Canada. I lived in Canada for two years. My son David was born in Canada. In 1970 I relocated to America with my two sons as an immigrant from Canada. Donald, their father, applied for permanent U.S. residence. (Donald had adopted Roger.) We hired a lawyer, and after a ten-year process, we received the visas, one for him, my two sons, and me.

I was divorced in 1977. I became a single working mother with three young children. I focused on taking care of myself and of them. I had permanent residency and the chance to work and enjoy life, but I came to America unsettled. Still, I adjusted and accepted and was satisfied with my life in America. I gave no thought to becoming a citizen. As a permanent resident, I was eligible for naturalization after five years. I could apply to become a US citizenship, but I didn't apply until after seventeen years. My son Roger called me one day and asked me if I was a citizen. He had relocated to Japan and was living in Japan. I said no, and he encouraged me to apply for citizenship. I took his advice. I went to the immigration department and filed for naturalization. I filed the N-400 application for naturalization form and received a receipt with a date for an interview as part of the naturalization process. The interviewer asked for my birth certificate. I didn't have a need for it before. I had never applied for one. I didn't have a birth certificate with me, and I was given another appointment to complete the process.

I sent a letter to my mother in Trinidad and asked her to send me my birth certificate. She went to the registry of birth and requested the birth certificate. She gave my name Joyce, my date of birth, her name, her place of work, and other documentation, which was all correct on the registry, but there was no Joyce on the registry. Instead, Grace was on the birth record. My mother was asked to swear that Grace and Joyce were the same person. She received the birth certificate with the name Grace and mailed it to me. And that was how, and when, I learned my name was Grace and always had been. I was called Joyce from birth by my family, my aunts and uncles, and by everyone who knew me (and still am by some), but Joyce wasn't my name.

To my mother I remained Joyce and she called me that until she passed away many years later. It wasn't an easy adjustment for her after the many years that she had called me Joyce. I was christened and confirmed as Joyce. But where did Joyce come from? Or Grace? Neither is a family name. Why was I called Joyce by my grandmother, my mother, and by every member of the family and not Grace? I began to remember stories that I had heard about my family and the way things were done in those days. My mother's sister-in-law, her first brother's wife, whom I called Nini, was the person who took care of the family's affairs. When there was a birth, a death, or any family event, she was the person who made the arrangements, and she also was the midwife who delivered the babies.

My mother didn't know that my name was Grace. She didn't register me at birth, and it might have been Nini who registered me as Grace and forgot to tell my mother. Somehow I was Joyce and Joyce I remained until I became a U.S. citizen thirty-two years later. At that time the baby, that's me, was called Joyce by all the family members and maybe she didn't mention the name Grace that she had given to the registry of birth. At that time, the registry registered new births, but didn't issue a birth certificate unless requested. Back in the U.S., I returned as scheduled to the USCIS office with my new birth certificate to complete my application to be naturalized, and on it I changed my name from Joyce to Grace, explaining that I wanted to have the name on my birth certificate. I answered the civil questions correctly and was soon notified that I was eligible for naturalization, with the time, date, and location for my naturalization oath ceremony.

On the day of the ceremony I turned in my green card. There were hundreds of people that day in 1997 in the auditorium, and we all took the oath of allegiance to

become a US citizen. I received my certificate of naturalization, in the name of Grace, and a US flag. I left and
celebrated that day with a friend. From Joyce to Grace, I
had a new identity, but it took me years to complete the
changeover. Everyone knew me as Joyce and all my docu-
ments were in that name, which I changed. Even so, some
still call me by my old name—but that's all right! They
had become accustomed to Joyce and didn't like the idea
of remembering a new name, and I tell the story over and
over how Joyce wasn't my name and how I became Grace.

Friendship

As a child, I was very quiet and I loved to read. Most of the time I had a book. I didn't have many friends; books were my friend and I'd read for hours. Once when I was reading, Tanty said, "Get to bed," and she turned off the lights. But the house we lived in was just boards and I could read by the moonlight coming through the cracks. Many nights I stayed up reading into the early morning.

One of my good friends was Lorna Joseph when I lived on Lastique Street, East Dry River. We were next-door neighbors and both in the eighth grade. I trusted her and felt safe in her company. On moonlit nights and even on dark nights when the stars shone brightly and glittered in the sky we would sit talking, many times until after midnight. Tanty took me out of school after the eighth grade and I got job as a helper in the kitchen of a nearby cafe.

Then at fifteen I got pregnant. I was devastated. I didn't tell my friend, Lorna, that I was pregnant, or that I was going away to live with my mother in Chaguanas. I left. I just disappeared without a trace. It wasn't something that I had expected to happen to me. The memory of leaving and not letting her know that I wasn't coming back brought a sadness to me. I left Lastique Street in 1960 and didn't go back to visit until 1980. In those twenty years I had three children, was married and divorced, had moved from Chaguanas to Port of Spain, then to Canada and the U.S. I asked my aunt Evelyn about Lorna but she said Lorna had gone to America and she didn't know where. That was fifty-nine years ago as I write this memoir.

Planned untimeliness is one of my peeves. An event is set to start at seven o'clock; I show up at that time, but the event itself won't start for almost another hour. Meanwhile I and anyone else who was on time have to wait. That's not real, but it's the practice in many places.

But I am still punctual. I get uncomfortable and I do not like it if I am late—or if someone else is late. A fifteen years' friendship has helped me with this. Rosemary, that friend, is a successful independent businesswoman, originally from Nigeria, who for years has operated her own hair and beauty salon, as well as raising by herself as a single mom four strong and independent children. We first met at church—how many true and enduring friends are found at church!—and spoke and from time to time helped each other. Rose finds time for active participation in her community, even being at one time the president of the Nigerian Association of Merrimack Valley, and a delegate to a "leadership exchange" with a Rwandan youth organization. As it happens, however, she is rarely on time, and I have learned to accept it, out of love and respect for her. At first when she'd be late, I would worry and fret, but I learned that in every case there was nothing for me to worry about; if nothing else she is always extremely busy. And from this experience with my friend

I learn to be more relaxed about time and myself. We understand each other. I know she may be late, and for my sake she tries not to be, and together we are patient with each other and are good friends.

I've known my friend Gloria for twenty-five years. We met at a Faith Fellowship Ministry church prayer meeting where we were the only two who attended, so we prayed together. She was new to the church. We hadn't spoken before. We started talking about things we liked to do, our purpose, and our shared desire to help people in need. When we left we exchanged phone numbers and we became sister friends. At Faith Fellowship Ministry we attended their school-year Advanced Leadership Training program.

Grace and Gloria at graduation

I needed a ride to attend the training and Gloria brought me and took me home, many miles out of her way, but without her help I could neither have attended nor completed it. We completed it together and graduated. We then went together with our class to Ghana in West Africa on the mission field to help children in need, as we had discussed when we first met in the prayer room. Gloria has a heart's desire to help as many people as she can, including me when I have needed it, even on one occasion taking me to the airport for a 5:00 a.m. flight. We have built a strong bond of sister friendship. We trust and are there for each other, and sometimes we reminisce about those times.

I knew Dallas for thirty years. We met while we were single parents raising our children and working to make a living. I was working at University hospital in Boston, and she worked as an administrative assistant. Her office was located next to the hospital, and every day Dallas came to the hospital mailing room to get the mail.

One day as she was walking to get her mail, she saw me and said hello. We talked for a short while and there was sense of us knowing each other in a friendly way. We often saw each other in passing and would say hello. Eventually we exchanged phone number and we connected. She lived in Cambridge, Massachusetts and I lived in Winchester. She had two children and I had three, about the same age as hers, and we vacationed together with our children in Maine. We had many wonderful sister friendship times that to tell of would take up most of these pages.

Dallas and I attended and were members of the same church for many years, Faith Fellowship Ministry in Winchester, Massachusetts (now International Family Church in Reading). We completed their two years of study in Bible school training. Then she went back to school to get her MA in education and became an English teacher at the church's Agape Faith Fellowship Ministry School, an accredited K-8 private school. She was from Nova Scotia and I was from Trinidad. We both had the experience of starting new lives and we had many discussions about remarriage, her birth place and mine, and about our hopes for the future. I met her mother and a few of her siblings. We were from different parents, but we had a sister connection that was very rare.

Then we lost track of each other for several years. I didn't know if she was living in Massachusetts or whether she had gone back to Nova Scotia, and I had moved and was living in Lowell, Massachusetts. I was divorced in 1977. I didn't have a happy marriage, and I had a desire to marry again. The experience I had in marriage wasn't how a marriage should be, and I knew in my heart that marriage was better than what I had experienced. I accepted salvation in 1983, and began to see life differently. I read in the Bible: "A man should leave his father and mother and cleave to his wife and they two shall be one flesh." God is the author of marriage and not of confusion, neither strife nor brutality but of peace. I desired what I had read in the Bible, and I wanted that in a marriage. I prayed and asked God to let me know if I will be married again, and if not, I was prepared to live single. I waited to hear from God, and I received an answer. In my heart, I had such peace, and in my inner being, I knew the answer was yes. I didn't know the day or the time, but I was satisfied with the answer, and I continued to immerse myself in the word of God and the teaching that I was receiving from the different ministries. I was so happy with myself and the new life I was experiencing in God. I made a vision book in a photo album with pictures of the gown that I would like to wear on my wedding day, and I wrote scriptures and positive affirmation, his qualities, his values, his beliefs, where I was weak that he may be strong in those qualities to name a few. My vision book wasn't only my vision but also that I believed I will marry again

I was working as a case manager with a government program that provided part-time work for persons over 55 while they looked for a permanent full-time job. Timothy was a participant in the program and I was his case manager. Soon enough he found a job, but before he started he invited me out to have dinner with him. I told him I was busy and didn't accept his invitation. Six months later he asked me out again. This time I accepted. I had been invited to a play the following week in the evening, *Fufu and Oreos*, created and performed by Obehi Janice, Rose's daughter. I invited him and he accepted.

He picked me up, we went to the play, and after we left the play we had a late dinner at a local restaurant. After that he took me home; I invited him to attend a church service with me on the following Sunday, and we attended church that Sunday. That was twenty-eight years after I received an answer from God that I would marry again, that I met the man who would be my husband. When we were married after a year, I reminded him that I had said I was busy the first time he asked me out, and he said, "You didn't say no."

We met in May 2011. We spoke daily and went out to dinner regularly. We took road trips to Maine, for the ride, the beaches, the cold water, the shopping, and just to drive and be together. Three months after we met, he asked me to marry him, and I said yes! I was engaged to be married, and I wanted to share this experience with my friend, Dallas. We had talked about remarrying again and wanting to be a maid of honor in each other's wedding, and I wanted her to be in my wedding and be my maid of honor.

I didn't know where she lived. I tried asking people who had known her but without success and it seemed like it wasn't to be. Several weeks before the wedding, I did get a reply from one of her friends who gave me her email address. I was so happy I couldn't wait to let her know that I was engaged and our talk about remarrying again had come true for me. I sent her an email and waited for her reply. She responded right away, and she was very happy for me. We set a day and time to meet at a restaurant and were reunited in friendship. She told me that she lived in nearby Reading, Massachusetts. I asked her to be my maid of honor, and she was delighted and remembered our discussion on honoring each other on that day. I hadn't done anything in preparing for the wedding.

I believed I would marry again, but I had no knowledge of how to plan a wedding. I was attending Whole Armour International Church in Lowell, Massachusetts, and I made an appointment with the pastor there to officiate the wedding and to schedule a wedding date. He gave me two dates to choose from and I chose Saturday, July 7, 2012. I had previously picked out a wedding gown before I heard from Dallas, and it was on layaway at the bridal shop. I took Dallas to the bridal shop and showed her my wedding bridal gown, and she loved it. She selected a beautiful dress to wear on my wedding day as the maid of honor. Dallas selected our wedding invitations cards and my fiancé and I wrote on them the words, "We are vowing to make it last forever." When they were done, Dallas got them and she mailed them out.

We went to the bridal shop and took the gown out of layaway and hid it from my fiancé at Dallas's apartment. We told him how beautiful the gown was, but we didn't want him to see it before I walked down the aisle wearing the gown on the wedding day.

We arranged for a reception hall and a host-DJ, selecting the function room, seating, menu, and music we liked, and making the necessary deposits. Then I got cold feet and everything was cancelled! Ten days later my fiancé still wanted to marry me, and so Dallas and I restarted our planning. For our reception we decided to "take over" a very nice buffet-style Indian restaurant - and they agreed to be taken over. The tables were arranged in a long-table sitting, everyone sitting together, and able to serve themselves as much as they wanted from a selection of delicious Indian food. It was a less formal reception that worked very well! Dallas and I then resumed our planning, meeting weekly to go over the arrangements for the wedding itself, and I selected the bride entrance songs and incidental music to be played at the church. In fact, Dallas herself did much of the planning, with me helping and agreeing.

My son, Roger, lives in Japan, and he came to the US to attend the wedding with his wife and my grandson, Ra, and he walked me down the aisle. My son, David, was best man, and my fiancé's niece a bridesmaid. Jesse, my grandson, was an escort, and my daughter, Debra, attended. We had breakfast rehearsal reception on Friday morning and were married Saturday, July 7, 2012. On that Friday evening

Dallas brought from her home the wedding dress that she'd kept hidden for two weeks, along with her own things, and she slept over that night. I hadn't tried it on again before she brought it over. That night I went to bed around ten o'clock. At ten-thirty, I awoke with a scary thought, "What if the gown doesn't fit?" I rushed to the guest room where Dallas was sleeping, woke her up, and said to her, "Dallas, what if the gown can't fit me." She got up and we took the gown off the hanger and I tried it on. It fit perfectly and I went back to bed and to sleep.

The next morning after we had breakfast we drove to my friend Rose's beauty salon and had our hair styled. After we left the hairdresser we went to the florist and picked up the boutonniere for the groomsmen and the male ushers. I had reserved the dressing room at the church for the bridal party. The ceremony was at 4:00, and the guest arrival time at 3:00. Dallas and I went to the church and I changed into my wedding gown, and she into her gown. The bridesmaids arrived. All were in attendance and the guests were seated.

The music started, the ceremony began. With the pastor, my son, David, the best man, stood with the groom at the front as the bridal party entered and proceeded down the center aisle, I on my son's arm, bridesmaids behind.

The music started with "Here Comes the Bride" but I had arranged for it to quickly change to the song, "My God is Awesome." As my son and I passed, the guests stood. My fiancé reached his hand out and took mine in his as the pastor asked who gave this woman to be married to this man. Roger said, "I do," and sat down, and the service began. That was seven years ago. Our marriage is blessed and grows stronger day by day. God is faithful with what he promises. He certainly is able to accomplish. Dallas is a friend forever, although our friendship on earth was interrupted by her death too soon a few years later. It was designed by our Heavenly Father God, and that kind of friendship never dies. It lives forever. We are friends forever.

Grace, the bride

My son Roger escorting his mom.
Background, Obehi Janice, playwright
and daughter of a friend.

Pastor Anthony Triplett, bride and
groom, and best man David.

Mother and Roger

Bride and groom, Grace and Timothy

Left to right: Debra, Dallas, Ayako holding her
son Ra, behind the bride Jesse (my grandson), the
bride and groom, Liz in front of the groom, David
and Roger behind Liz, and Kelsey to the right.

Bride and Dallas, maid of honor

Maid of honor, Dallas with bride and
groom, Grace and Timothy

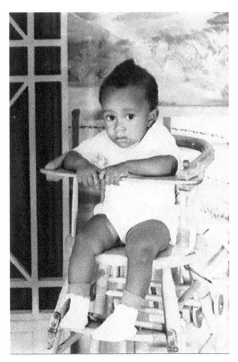

Dexter Calvin Neils, my first son

Dexter grown to be an adult. He worked as a
security officer for over twenty-five years.
He passed away in 2014 at the age of fifty-two years.

Feelings Recovered Summary

I didn't know that I was damaged. On the surface, I function just fine, always had a smile on my face, which was genuine. The experience I had of being raped three times and molested and the babies that I had aborted, I didn't know then how it would affect me as an adult. I wasn't aware of the emotional pain that I carried for all those years until I made the decision to write my autobiography. When I began writing my memoir, I broke down with tears at the emotional pain I felt from the memories of my experiences and the hurt that was imbedded within me. I couldn't continue to go on writing and I took time off from writing. I spoke then to my friend Andrea, saved with me in 1983 and whom I have known for many years. I told her about the experience and effect of the emotional pain and she said to me, "That's why you always looked so sad, and only when you talked about Jesus, you lit up and looked happy." Soon after, I started with counseling, which has helped me in overcoming the emotional pain and sadness of my childhood. Regular meetings with my therapist over time made a difference in that now I am able to release that sadness and pain from my childhood, and through her help I am learning that my past doesn't need to control my life and my future. I am now able to choose the life I want to live and that sadness and pain are no longer a part of it. I was saved, but within me emotionally, there were issues that had to be addressed. I was functioning consciously, and I didn't know there was subconscious emotional pain locked within my subconscious mind through life experiences. I had gone to parties before I was saved, and dancing made me feel good, but the feeling was momentary only temporary, and after I went home, the feelings was gone and replaced with sadness.

About the Author

Minister Grace Neils Woodbridge was born in 1945 in the Caribbean, in Petersfield, Chaguanas, Trinidad and Tobago. She is of African Caribbean and Indian ethnicity; the first child born to Christine Neils Gould and Ishmael Hamilton. She attended Cambridge College in Cambridge, Massachusetts. She graduated from Faith Fellowship Ministry Victory Bible School and also their School of Advanced Leadership Training. She is an ordained minister and member of the National Association of Christian Ministers (NACM).

Minister Grace, also known as Joyce, was a missionary for six months in 1992 at New Mission in Leogane, Haiti. There she supervised the school feeding program. In 2000 she was a missionary in Accra, Ghana, West Africa, where she assisted a medical team that brought medicines to treat those sick with severe medical conditions in Tamale village and visited the schools with supplies in the town of Dodowa. She is a certified marriage and pre-marriage coach, as well as an evangelist and teacher of the ministry of the Word of God via reconciliation with an emphasis on salvation. Ethnicity; African Caribbean descendant of Benin. Minister Grace gave birth to Dexter, Roger, David, and Debra. She has three grandchildren, Jesse, Ra, and Nia, and is married to Timothy Woodbridge, the stepfather of her children. She lives in Tyngsborough, Massachusetts.

She was sedated by life trauma, living life but life wasn't in her. She was suppressed. She couldn't cry. She blocked her feelings. She didn't want to feel pain. She couldn't feel joy and didn't know what happiness was. She could give, but she didn't know how to receive. She has a spirit. She has a soul, and she lives in a body. She is saved, but her soul isn't. It is being saved. She was emotionally affected, and it wasn't until she had addressed the pain within her, released the anger, the hurt from feelings of abandonment, the rejection, sadness, and her anxieties, that she was able to feel her feelings, experience joy, feel happiness, and trust people. Her soul is being saved and the healing continues. *The Word of God is alive and powerful. It is sharper than the sharpest two-edged sword. It penetrates even to dividing soul and spirit. The Word of God planted in her which can save her soul.* Hebrews 4:12, James 1:21